How to Play a Good Game of Bridge

Terence Reese has been a professional bridge player for over thirty years and is equally well known as a player, author, journalist and broadcaster. He is the bridge correspondent for the *Observer*, the *Evening News* and *The Lady*. Albert Dormer is a chartered surveyor by profession. He has an international reputation as a bridge correspondent and commentator and edits many of the daily bulletins published at European Championships and World Olympiads.

Terence Reese and Albert Dormer have collaborated on several books, including *The Acol System Today*.

Also available in Pan Books

Bridge for Beginners
Victor Mollo and Nico Gardener

Common-Sense Bridge
Rixi Marcus

HOW TO PLAY A
GOOD GAME OF BRIDGE

TERENCE REESE
and
ALBERT DORMER

Pan Books in association with William Heinemann

First published 1969 by William Heinemann Ltd
This edition published 1971 by Pan Books Ltd,
Cavaye Place, London SW10 9PG,
in association with William Heinemann Ltd
4th Printing 1975
©Terence Reese and Albert Dormer 1969
ISBN 0 330 02790 5

Made and printed in Great Britain by
Cox & Wyman Ltd, London, Reading and Fakenham

Contents

Foreword

Bridge is a game with an elaborate technique both of bidding and play, and there are numerous textbooks (we have contributed our share) dealing with these subjects. Here we have adopted a rather different scheme. The combined point count which we describe in Chapter One, and the tables at the end, provide a standard of reference for all common situations in bidding. Thereafter, the book is a commentary rather than a technical account. We deal with broad subjects such as when to bid No Trumps rather than a suit, how to choose between biddable suits, how to exploit a part score, how to do the right thing in a competitive auction.

As every player knows, there are many different styles and systems of bidding, some suitable for duplicate, some for the cut-in game. We have not paused to discuss points of theory. The method we describe is easy to play and will serve well for rubber bridge at any level.

Terence Reese
Albert Dormer

Part One

The Opening Side

CHAPTER 1

How to Value Your Hand

*Combined point count – How to acquire expert judge-
ment – Summary – Point count requirements*

BRIDGE has never been quite the same since players learned
to count points for distribution as well as for high cards.

As every player knows from experience, the strength of a
hand depends as much on the distributional pattern as on
the high cards. The two act together, almost like a chemical
combination. It is not always easy to gauge the net effect.
But it is a lot easier than it used to be before 'combined
point count' was developed.

Before the invention of a combined count a beginner had
to be talented – or thick-skinned – to survive. Many found
the game too difficult and gave up. Then a method publi-
cized by the American writer, Charles Goren, transformed
the whole situation. Taking the already familiar 4-3-2-1
count for high cards, he showed how to add points for
distribution. A hand could then be said to be worth so-many
points 'including distribution'. Players found this method
greatly to their liking and bridge is a more popular game
because of it.

Today nearly all beginners learn to value their hands by
means of a combined count – not necessarily Goren's. They
reach reasonable contracts from the start and still better
contracts as they acquire judgement. This takes time, and
meanwhile the combined count is a very good guide indeed.

There are several popular ways of counting points, differ-
ing only in detail. Whichever method you use, you will find
that if you and your partner hold less than 26 points it will

be advisable to drop the bidding in a safe part score. With 26 to 32 points you should bid a game, and with 33 or more you are in the slam zone.

The particular method of valuation which we describe has the advantage of giving more accurate results than any other on unbalanced hands, which are usually the ones most difficult to assess.

COMBINED POINT COUNT

Count first your high-card points.

Ace	=	4 points
King	=	3 points
Queen	=	2 points
Jack	=	1 point

To your high-card points you now add points for distribution, as follows:

Add 1 point each for the fifth and sixth card in any suit, 2 points for each subsequent card.

The following hand contains 15 points – 14 for high cards, 1 for the fifth heart.

♠ K J 5   ♡ A Q 10 6 2   ◇ A 9 7   ♣ 10 4

In the same way, if your hand contained two five-card suits, or a six-card suit, you would add 2 distributional points. A seven-card suit is worth 4 distributional points.

♠ A 8   ♡ A 10 8 7 5 3 2   ◇ A Q 2   ♣ 10

This hand has a count of 18 points in all.
Before reading further, commit these landmarks to mind:

To open with a bid of One you need 13 points including distribution. (A hand with 12 points in high cards and none for distribution is a borderline opening.)

To respond at the One level you need 6 points including distribution; at the Two level, 9 points.

To make game in a major suit you need 26 points in the two hands. You normally need the same number for a game in No Trumps, but if you can count at least 25 in high cards it is a fair speculation to bid game rather than 'hang' in Two No Trumps.

On page 21 the vital statistics for every bid in a normal auction are set out in terms of points.

The responder can count his points in just the same way as the opening bidder.

♠ Q 9 7 5 3   ♡ Q J 4   ◇ 8 2   ♣ 9 7 6

Holding 6 points, including 1 for the fifth card in his long suit, responder is just worth a One-over-One bid in spades.

When you are opening the bidding, or responding in a new suit, the task of counting points is as simple as that. But when your side has found a playable trump suit further adjustments are needed. This is because trick-winning power increases sharply when there is an eight-card or longer trump suit, shared fairly evenly between the two hands. To reflect this increased power you must add extra points whenever the bidding reveals that such a trump suit exists.

Suppose your partner opens One Heart and you hold this hand:

♠ A 10   ♡ K J 5 3   ◇ Q 10 7 4 3   ♣ 9 4

Normally this would be worth 11 points – 10 for high cards and 1 for the fifth diamond. But as you intend to play in hearts – a suit in which the partnership must hold at least eight cards – you can add 'support points' according to this scale:

> *Add 1 point for each doubleton in a side suit.*
> *Add 2 points for each singleton.*
> *Add 3 points for a void.*

The hand above, with its two doubletons, is worth 2 more points – 13 in all. As opener's expected minimum is 13 there will be at least 26 in the combined hands. Responder may therefore raise his partner's One Heart opening to Four Hearts.

Support points may be added only by the player who first supports his partner's trump suit. This will not necessarily be the responder. On this next hand the opener may add support points because he intends to raise the responder's suit.

♠ A Q 4 2   ♡ 6   ♢ A K J 9 2   ♣ Q J 8

Opener bids One Diamond and his partner responds One Spade. Opener started out with 18 points, including distribution. Now he can add 2 points for the singleton heart. Responder's minimum is 6, so the total is 26 and opener is worth a raise to Four Spades.

The combined count works equally well when either player is considering a bid in No Trumps after the bidding has been opened in a suit. The 26-point guide line for a game contract still holds good. Suppose you are the responder on the following hand:

Opener	Responder
1 ♠	2 ♣
2 ♠	

Responder holds: ♠ 8 2 ♡ Q 9 8 4 ♢ K 3 ♣ A Q 10 4 2

The natural move on the responding hand is a bid of No Trumps, and the question is, how many?

Opener's simple rebid of Two Spades indicates a minimum hand of 13 to 15 points, including distribution. The responding hand is worth 12 points, including distribution. As there may be less than 26 points in the combined hands and there is no guarantee of a fit in clubs, the recommended bid is Two No Trumps, which opener will raise if his hand is in the upper bracket.

HOW TO ACQUIRE EXPERT JUDGEMENT

On hands where the final contract can be reached in two or three bids, straightforward application of combined point count may supply all the answers. On others, of course, there is more to it. Several suits may be mentioned, and as new information comes in, the good player will make adjustments to the value of his hand. The most important factor is that high-card points tend to be worth more than their face value when held in a suit which the partnership expects to establish. They may also be worth either more or less than their face value when held in a suit which has been bid by the opposition. In this last case much may depend on the *location* of the cards. Clearly a holding such as K J x is worth much more sitting over the opponent's call than sitting under it.

Skill in bidding depends in the long run on how well you assess factors of that kind. With a little experience counting points is automatic, and with a little more experience systemic errors should be infrequent. The player who goes on from there to become a really good bidder is the one who is sensitive to the finer points that we are now going to describe.

The majority of contracts cannot be made just by cashing high cards: it is nearly always necessary to establish some long cards. It is easier to do this when the long cards are held in the same suit as one or more high cards. This factor may sometimes be taken into account as early as the opening bid.

♠ A   ♡ 10 7 5 4 3   ◇ Q 8 7 2   ♣ K Q J

With 13 points this is theoretically worth opening, but it is in fact much weaker than most 13-point hands because the points are held in short suits and do not accompany the length. There is something rather impressive about a singleton Ace, but it is really quite a poor holding. One would much rather transfer the Ace from spades to hearts.

Of course, it is just as valuable to hold high cards in your partner's suits as in your own. This factor should sway the decision on a hand like this:

♠ Q J 6 4 3 2   ♡ 2   ◇ A Q 5   ♣ J 10 2

Opener	Responder
1 ♣	1 ♠
2 ♠	?

On this hand you are the responder. Partner opens One Club and you bid One Spade, which he raises to Two Spades. Question: do you go straight to game?

As you hold 12 points, including distribution, it appears that if opener is minimum you will total only 25 points, not enough for game. However, a decision as close as this should be swayed by judgement rather than by arithmetic. Specifically, you should place an enhanced value on the club holding simply because your partner has bid that suit. J 10 x will be a distinct asset, certainly worth more than 1 point, opposite any biddable club suit in partner's hand. Therefore you should bid game.

If partner had opened One Heart instead of One Club and had raised One Spade to Two Spades you would have been worth a bid of only Three Spades. The singleton heart would not help you to develop tricks in partner's main suit.

This touches on one of the finer points of hand valuation. The number of cards held in partner's suit is important, as well as the rank. The best holding is a doubleton honour, for this suggests no losers and at the same time good prospects of establishing the long cards. A low doubleton is promising too, and a singleton is better than a void. A small trebleton is a particularly bad holding when a slam in a suit is under consideration, but not when game in No Trumps is the objective. Three rag cards opposite partner's holding of A x x x x would give him an excellent chance of making three tricks in the suit at No Trumps but would obviously be a millstone in a slam contract, even if this were only a side suit.

When there has been competitive bidding it is especially

important to consider whether your high cards are likely to be well or badly placed in relation to the opponent's holdings. On the following hand you open with a bid of One Spade:

♠ A K 7 5 3   ♡ A 5 2   ◇ 10 9 4   ♣ K 6

Suppose, first, that there is a butt-in of Two Clubs on your left. Whatever happens after that, you should treat your hand as a minimum unless you propose to become the declarer at No Trumps. If the club bid had been on your right the King of clubs would be almost equal to an Ace.

Harder to assess is 'duplication'. The partners may both be short in the same suit or their points may overlap. Suppose you hold K Q 10 opposite partner's A J x: with 10 points you can make only three tricks. This is poor value, for the Jack and 10 are wasted and there are no long cards to be promoted.

A player who can spot the duplication bug is on the way to becoming a very skilled bidder. Watch out for sequences like this:

Opener	Responder
1 NT	?

Responder holds: ♠ A K J ♡ J 9 ◇ 8 7 5 2 ♣ J 7 4 2

The honours in spades do not accompany length and quite possibly face Q x x in the opener's hand. For the purpose of supporting One No Trump the whole hand should be treated as worth about 8 points, not 10.

It is equally bad for both partners to have the same shortage. When both opponents bid your short suit you must appreciate that partner may also hold a doubleton or singleton.

To sum up, it is proper to value your hand by means of point count for the first round or two. As the bidding develops you must rely more on judgement. Counting points doesn't make you a good bidder. Making intelligent adjustments, in the way we have described, does.

SUMMARY

In the early rounds rely on combined point count, adding 1 point each for the fifth and sixth, 2 points for the seventh card in any suit. When supporting with four trumps count 1, 2, 3 points for doubleton, singleton, void.

Open with 13 points, respond with 6. Bid game with 26, slam with 33.

As the bidding progresses, look for signs of a good or bad fit.

POINT COUNT REQUIREMENTS

These tables are for reference. Don't try to master all the figures at this stage.

THE POINTS YOU NEED TO OPEN THE BIDDING

OPENING BID	QUALIFICATIONS
One No Trump	15 to 17 points, balanced hand
One in a suit	13 to 20 points
Two No Trumps	20 to 22 points, balanced hand
Two Clubs	23 points up, balanced hand, *or* 21 points up, powerful distribution
Two Diamonds, Two Hearts, Two Spades	18 to 22 points, at least eight playing tricks
Three No Trumps	Solid minor suit, little else
Three in a suit	Seven playing tricks if vulnerable, six if not vulnerable, less than 13 points
Four in a suit	Eight playing tricks if vulnerable, seven if not vulnerable, less than 13 points

THE POINTS YOU NEED TO RESPOND

OPENING BID	RESPONSE	QUALIFICATIONS
One No Trump	Pass (or sign-off in Two Diamonds, Two Hearts or Two Spades)	0 to 8 points
	Two No Trumps	9 to 10 points
	Three No Trumps	11 to 15 points
	Four No Trumps (not forcing)	16 to 17 points
	Two Clubs (Stayman)	Any strength, playable in a 4-4 fit
	Three in a suit	11 points up
	Slam bid or slam investigation	18 points up
One in a suit	Pass	0 to 5 points
	One-level response in a new suit	6 to 15 points
	Two-level response in a new suit	9 to 15 points
	One No Trump	6 to 9 points, fairly balanced
	Two No Trumps	11 to 12 points, fairly balanced

OPENING BID	RESPONSE	QUALIFICATIONS
One in a suit (continued)	Three No Trumps	13 to 15 points, completely balanced
	Jump shift in new suit (single jump)	16 points up
	Pre-emptive response in new suit (double jump)	Weak hand, seven-card suit
	Raise of opener's suit	*(With four-card support, add to the previous value of your hand: 3 for a void, 2 for a singleton, 1 for a doubleton)*
	Single raise	6 to 9 points
	Double raise	10 to 12 points, at least four trumps
	Raise to game	13 to 15 points, at least four trumps
Two No Trumps	Pass	0 to 3 points
	Three Clubs	4 points up, playable in a 4-4 fit
	Three Diamonds, Three Hearts, Three Spades	4 points up, five-card suit
	Three No Trumps	4 to 10 points
	Four Hearts, Four Spades	4 to 10 points, six-card suit
	Four No Trumps	11 to 12 points
	Slam bid or slam investigation	13 points up

OPENING BID	RESPONSE	QUALIFICATIONS
Two Clubs	Two Diamonds	0 to 7 points
	Two No Trumps	8 to 10 points, no biddable suit
	Two Hearts, Two Spades, Three Clubs, Three Diamonds	8 points up, biddable suit
Two Diamonds, Two Hearts, Two Spades	Two No Trumps	0 to 9 points
	Simple bid in new suit	7 points up at Two level 10 points up at Three level
	Single raise of opener's suit	7 points up, including an Ace
	Double raise of opener's suit	9 to 12 points, no Ace

Responses to other opening bids are based on judgement, not specifically on point count.

THE POINTS FOR OPENER'S SECOND BID
following an opening of One in a suit

RESPONDER'S BID	OPENER'S BID	QUALIFICATIONS
New suit at One level	One No Trump	13 to 14 points, fairly balanced
	Two No Trumps	18 to 19 points, fairly balanced
	Three No Trumps	20 points up, fairly balanced
	Simple rebid in original suit	13 to 16 points, good five-card suit
	Simple bid in new suit	13 to 19 points
	Jump to Three in opener's suit	17 to 19 points, six-card suit
	Jump to Four in opener's suit	20 points, strong six-card suit
	Jump shift in new suit (forcing)	20 points up (may include 'support' points)
	Raise of responder's suit (Include 'support' points)	
	Single raise	13 to 16 points
	Double raise	17 to 19 points
	Raise to game	20 points up

RESPONDER'S BID	OPENER'S BID	QUALIFICATIONS
New suit at Two level (not a jump)	Two No Trumps	15 to 17 points
	Three No Trumps	18 points up
	Simple bid in new suit or rebid of original suit	13 to 16 points
	Bid of Three in new suit (forcing)	17 points up
Raise of responder's suit (Add support points)		
	Single raise	13 to 16 points
	Double raise (forcing if responder has bid a minor suit)	17 points up
One No Trump	Pass	13 to 16 points, fairly balanced
	Two in a suit	13 to 16 points, unbalanced
	Raise to Two No Trumps	17 to 18 points
	Raise to Three No Trumps, or jump bid in suit	19 points up
Jump shift in new suit (single jump, forcing)	Minimum rebid in No Trumps	13 to 14 points
	Jump to Three No Trumps (over response at Two level)	15 to 17 points
	All other bids	13 points up

CHAPTER 2

Which Suit to Bid

Balanced hands – Unbalanced hands – When partner has passed – The choice of suit on big hands – Responder's choice of suit – Summary

WHY do some players home on to the best contract as if guided by radar while others stagger from one bid to another and end up guessing? Answer: largely because they choose the correct suit to bid on the first round.

When a player opens with One of a suit he undertakes to find another bid if partner responds in a new suit. This second bid will not slot readily into place unless the first bid was right.

To plot the choice of suit properly you have to weigh up the various objectives and decide which of them count most on your particular hand.

> *You want to tell your partner as much – and the opponents as little – as possible.*
>
> *If the final contract is likely to be a trump suit you want that suit to be the longest combination in the two hands.*
>
> *Other things being equal, you would prefer your opening bid to be in a major suit, as the opponents will find this more difficult to overcall than a minor suit.*
>
> *If aiming no higher than game you should attach far more importance to the major suits than to the minors. But if a slam is possible the minor suits are just as important as the majors.*

A player who has these objectives in mind will be flexible and will reach sound decisions on hands where the choice of suit is debatable. He may bid the same type of hand differently with different partners. He will also know how to select his bids according to the state of the rubber.

BALANCED HANDS

You are more likely to hold a hand containing two four-card suits than any other type. And it will nearly always make a difference which of those suits you bid first. Much depends on the number of points you hold.

When you hold 18 points or more you will find that the choice of opening is not nearly so critical as with a weaker hand. The guiding principle with 18 points is very simple: try to organize so that you can jump in No Trumps to show the full strength of your balanced hand on the second round, making sure that you do not conceal a strong major suit en route.

♠ A K 10 3   ♡ K 3   ◇ K Q J 4   ♣ Q 10 3

Open One Spade. If partner shows a minimum of 9 points by responding at the Two level you can jump to Three No Trumps. If you were to open One Diamond and partner were to bid One Heart, showing a minimum of 6 points, you could jump to Two No Trumps but might now be missing a spade fit.

When you hold 15 to 17 points you should open One No Trump unless the make-up of the hand is distinctly unsuitable. (How to assess the suitability of a hand for No Trumps is discussed in the next chapter.) If One No Trump is ruled out you should organize the bidding so that on the second round you can either (1) rebid your suit, or (2) bid a new suit, or (3) bid Two No Trumps over a response at the Two level. You should avoid rebidding One No Trump as this suggests that you have opened on a minimum 13–14 points.

When you hold 13 or 14 points it becomes even more important to choose the right suit originally. Any misjudgement is liable to cost heavily later in the auction. The point to remember on this type of hand is that while it is proper to rebid One No Trump on the second round it is unsound to rebid Two No Trumps even when partner has responded at the Two level. To make sure you will not be in trouble on the second round with a 13- or 14-point hand, follow this scheme on the first round:

1. *With touching suits, open the higher-ranking.* With hearts and diamonds, for example, open One Heart. If the response is One No Trump you will pass, if One Spade you may raise the spades or rebid One No Trump; but if partner responds Two Clubs you can bid Two Diamonds and partner can then return to the first suit without raising the level of the bidding. The same principle holds good for 5-5 hands as well as 4-4: open the higher suit, irrespective of strength.

2. *With clubs and hearts, or clubs and spades, open One Club.* Depending on the response, you can either show your second suit at the One level or rebid One No Trump.

♠ 8 7 2   ♡ A J 8 4   ◇ A 6   ♣ K J 4 2

Provided he opens One Club, opener can show his heart suit over a response of One Diamond or bid One No Trump over a response of One Spade. An opening bid of One Heart would create an embarrassment if partner responded in diamonds.

3. *With spades and diamonds, open the suit below the doubleton.* The worst that can happen now is that you may have to raise partner's suit with only three-card support.

♠ Q J 8 6   ♡ 7 4   ◇ A Q 10 2   ♣ K J 3

Open One Diamond. Over One Heart you can respond One Spade, and Two Clubs you can raise to Three Clubs. To open One Spade might turn out a mistake, for you would have no sound rebid over a response of Two Hearts. Remember that Two No Trumps at this juncture would suggest 15 to 17 points.

Suppose you hold *three* four-card suits. No problem! Open the suit below the singleton.

(1) ♠ K 10 7 3   ♡ Q 10 8 5   ◇ 8   ♣ A K J 2
(2) ♠ 6   ♡ A 8 6 4   ◇ A J 9 2   ♣ A 10 9 6

On (1) open One Club, on (2) One Heart. This way, none of the suits will get 'lost' and you will always have a sound rebid.

When the singleton is in clubs it is normal to open One Spade, but when the spades are weak One Heart is also acceptable.

(3) ♠ Q 10 7 3   ♡ A K 7 2   ◇ K J 4 2   ♣ 6

Open One Heart and rebid Two Diamonds. You don't want to play in spades unless partner can mention the suit.

And what about a hand that is completely 'flat', 4-3-3-3? Your principal concern now is not to put yourself in a position where you will have no good rebid over a response at the level of Two. This will mean that on most such hands you will have to open with One Club, even though you may have only three.

♠ 10 6 4   ♡ A 10 8 6   ◇ K J 2   ♣ K Q 9

Open One Club. If you open One Heart and partner responds with Two of a minor you are stranded; at best, you would be obliged to raise, despite the lack of ruffing values.

You may be wondering what happens on the second round after you have opened a 'short club'. If partner responds One Diamond on the hand above, for example, do you bid One Heart or One No Trump?

There are two schools of thought about this, but the modern tendency is to prefer the rebid in No Trumps. It has been found that the other sequence is too stimulating to the responder's imagination. He may form a wrong picture of your hand, taking it to be unbalanced. The rebid in No Trumps avoids that danger and has the great advantage of telling partner that you hold precisely 13 or 14 points.

One further point: if partner raises your short club, don't panic and retreat to No Trumps. He will surely be unbalanced, with at least four clubs and a singleton somewhere.

UNBALANCED HANDS

These are hands which contain a five-card or longer suit. Actually, a 5-3-3-2 pattern is not unbalanced and may often be opened with a bid of One No Trump. Except for that, the five-card suit should always be named.

On hands containing a five-card suit and a four-card suit, it is normal to open the longer suit even if it is weaker in high cards. This is because in a trump contract the length of the combined trump holding is the most important factor.

There is one type of 5-4 hand, however, which must sometimes be treated differently. This is when the two suits are touching and the five-card suit is lower ranking. Say that you hold four hearts and five diamonds. A sequence such as One Diamond–One Spade–Two Hearts, where your second suit is higher ranking than the first, is called a 'reverse' and denotes at least 16 points. Thus on weaker hands a small conflict arises: either one of the suits must be suppressed or the four-card suit must be bid in front of the five-card suit. A few examples will show how the problem is resolved.

(1) ♠ 4   ♡ A 10 7 3   ◇ A Q J 9 6   ♣ J 8 6

Open One Diamond and, over One Spade or Two Clubs, rebid Two Diamonds. You don't mind suppressing the hearts.

(2) ♠ Q 4   ♡ A K J 6   ◇ K 10 7 5 2   ♣ 8 5

Open One Heart and follow with Two Diamonds on the next round. Partner won't know that you hold longer diamonds than hearts, but no matter.

(3) ♠ A 3   ♡ Q J 8 2   ◇ A Q 8 5 3   ♣ 10 6

Now it is a very moot point whether you should open One Diamond and rebid Two Diamonds, or open One Heart and follow with Two Diamonds. The disadvantage of this second course is that partner may give you jump preference in hearts with only three trumps. If you remember this example as a 'mid-way house' you will have a standard by which you can judge any other hand with similar distribution.

So far we have been considering the tamer type of hand pattern. Wilder patterns are potentially more powerful, but if you hold 'good shape' the other players will too. The auction may now become very competitive. On shapely hands which contain two suits it is usually advisable to open the higher-ranking, so that when you bid your second suit partner can return to the first without raising the level of the contract.

♠ 7   ♡ K 10 6 5 3   ◇ A 8   ♣ A K 5 4 2

It is better to open One Heart than One Club, as someone is likely to bid spades. You can then show the clubs and partner will be able to give preference at the same level. Even if opponents do not enter, it may be difficult to reach game in a 5-3 heart fit unless you bid the suit on the first round. Again:

♠ 4   ♡ A K J 5 2   ◇ K J 9 6 3 2   ♣ Q

This 16-point hand (counting the singleton Queen as 1 point only) is good enough for a One Diamond opening followed by a reverse bid in hearts. Unfortunately it is legal for the opponents to bid too – and on this type of deal they usually will. It may then be inconvenient to show hearts at all, let alone produce the finely-etched sequence that tells partner you hold six diamonds and five hearts. (In an un-contested auction you could achieve this by opening One Diamond and later bidding the hearts twice.) It will be better in practice to open One Heart and ensure that neither of your fine suits is frozen out.

A hand with five clubs and five spades provides an exception to the general rule of opening the higher suit with 5-5. Now One Club saves space and time.

WHEN PARTNER HAS PASSED

If you open the bidding in third or fourth position you are
not obliged to rebid over partner's response. This has little
practical importance if you are unbalanced, as you will then
be anxious to complete the picture. But on balanced hands
the fact that you can drop the bidding on the next round has
a simplifying effect, as a previous example will show.

♠ Q J 8 6   ♡ 7 4   ◇ A Q 10 2   ♣ K J 3

In first or second position we advised you to open One
Diamond so that you would have a sound rebid over any
response. Since in third or fourth position you are not
obliged to rebid, One Spade is permissible and even preferable, for this makes it more difficult for the opponents to
enter the auction. Finally:

♠ A K 4 2   ♡ J 9 4   ◇ Q 7 3   ♣ K J 10

Players who open One Club after a pass by partner have
presumably forgotten *why* it is ever necessary to bid a short
club. They fail to appreciate the virtue of opening a moderate
hand with a relatively high bid.

THE CHOICE OF SUIT ON BIG HANDS

A different touch may be needed when there is some prospect of a slam. We do not propose to spell this out in great
detail, for we think that two examples will shed sufficient
light.

♠ A 4   ♡ K 6 3 2   ◇ A Q 10 9   ♣ A Q 8

An opening bid of One Heart, the higher of adjacent suits,
would conform to theory. But is it sensible? If partner
supports hearts you will always be nervous about the trump
suit and will not be able to bid a slam with any confidence.
One Diamond is more intelligent. The lesson? Don't bid bad
suits on good hands when there is a chance you may finish
in a slam.

If partner has passed, you are not very likely to reach a slam and may be influenced by other tactical considerations.

♠ A Q   ♡ A 4 3 2   ◇ K J 7   ♣ A J 10 8

Open One Heart in third or fourth hand. This time One Club would be normal for dealer or second hand, but when the likely target is Three No Trumps it becomes silly to warn the opponents not to lead clubs. The fact that the heart suit is empty is no snag, as over a raise in hearts you intend to bid No Trumps. If partner persists in hearts, that may be the best contract.

RESPONDER'S CHOICE OF SUIT

Like the opening bidder, responder has to peer into the mists. With two biddable suits he must aim to leave himself comfortably placed on the second round. Partner opens One Diamond and you hold:

(1) ♠ K J 9 2   ♡ Q 10 8 4   ◇ 9 6   ♣ A J 3
(2) ♠ A Q 10 8   ♡ K Q 10 5   ◇ 7 6 4   ♣ 4 2

On the first hand respond One Heart. As you hold guards in the unbid suits you intend to rebid Two No Trumps over a Two Diamond rebid by partner. (There would be no point in showing spades, as opener would presumably bid that suit himself if he held it.) On most hands it is correct to bid in that fashion, making the cheapest One-over-One bid and providing the best chance to find a fit.

On the second hand there is a possible snag. If responder bids One Heart he will have an awkward decision to make over a rebid of Two Diamonds. Lacking a club guard he cannot bid Two No Trumps and a bid of Two Spades would suggest a five-card heart suit. Responder should therefore bid One Spade on the first round; then he can follow with Two Hearts.

Like the opener, responder will normally show his longest suit first, but this principle should be abandoned if it would

involve an unsound response at the Two level. Partner opens
One Heart and you hold:

     ♠ J 10 7 3   ♡ 4   ◇ A 8 5 3 2   ♣ J 6 2

It is inadvisable to respond Two Diamonds on this assortment. Bid One Spade and hastily pass a rebid of Two Hearts
– or of One No Trump or Two Clubs.

As you see, there are many rules for choosing the right
suit to bid. You don't have to remember any of them –
provided you make a habit of looking ahead and foreseeing
the snags.

SUMMARY

(a) *With only four-card suits.* With touching suits open the
higher-ranking. With diamonds and spades open the suit
below the doubleton (unless you are strong enough to rebid
Two No Trumps). With 4-4-4-1 open the suit below the
singleton. With other combinations open the lower suit on
weak hands, preferring a three-card minor with 4-3-3-3.

(b) *With 5-4* open the longer suit, except that with touching suits 4-5 it may be better to open the higher suit.

(c) *With 5-5* open the higher suit, except that you may
open One Club with five spades and five clubs.

(d) *With 6-5* normally open the longer suit, but prefer a
good five-card major to a broken six-card minor.

2-4c. Lower-ranking if divided.
Higher-. if adj.
Between 2-4c = which of the 2 others
you can support.

CHAPTER 3

When to Bid No Trumps

*When to bid game in No Trumps – The opening bid
of One No Trump – The Stayman convention – Other
responses to One No Trump – No Trump responses
to a suit opening – Summary*

IT is never necessary to bid No Trumps. There will always
be at least one other call you can make. But, given the
qualifications, it is desirable to bid No Trumps whenever
possible. These are some of the obvious virtues:

Nine tricks at No Trumps is the shortest route to game.
Any bid of No Trumps tells partner your hand within 1 or 2
points, enabling him to gauge the combined strength.
Finally, a bid of No Trumps leaves the opponents to guess
about suit lengths.

It is easy to calculate the right number of points for a bid
of No Trumps at any stage, and it is not difficult to decide
whether you hold a suitable pattern. Why, therefore, do
many players bid No Trumps when they ought to bid a suit –
or bid a suit when they ought to bid No Trumps? One
answer is that they do not appreciate the advantage of
having a set-up suit, another that they underrate the importance of tenace combinations, such as A Q x or K J x.

Tenace combinations are especially useful when held by
the declarer at No Trumps. It follows that when your hand
contains tenaces you should grab the chance to bid No
Trumps whenever possible. Conversely, if you hold no
tenaces you should give partner a chance to declare
No Trumps. Consider these two hands:

Opener	*Responder*
♠ A 7	♠ Q 3 2
♡ A 10 9 2	♡ J 5 3
◇ A 7 5 3	◇ K J 10
♣ A 3 2	♣ K J 9 6

The opener's hand is within the point-count range for One No Trump, and if that bid is chosen, partner will raise to Three No Trumps. If a spade is led and the King lies over the Queen, the contract may well fail. Declarer will draw attention to his 150 honours and it will not occur to him that he is in any way to blame.

As the <u>hand contains no tenaces</u> it is preferable to avoid opening One No Trump. Either One Heart or One Diamond is an acceptable opening. Responder will bid Two No Trumps and the final contract of Three No Trumps will be played from the right side.

There you have an example of the difference that good judgement makes in this particular field of bidding. We focus on this area for the remainder of the chapter.

WHEN TO BID GAME IN NO TRUMPS

Go for game in No Trumps whenever there are 26 points in two balanced hands. It is also a fair speculation to bid game on only 25 points if you are already at the Two level, for a contract of Two No Trumps will often depend on the same hazard as Three No Trumps, and of course the reward is less.

When the hands are slightly unbalanced – 4-4-3-2 or 5-4-2-2 – search for a 4-4 fit in a major suit. If none exists, bid game in No Trumps unless there is an obvious weakness in one suit.

It is not practical to wait for a guard in every suit. Take a chance that opponents won't be able to run five tricks, unless there has been an overcall and neither you nor your partner holds a guard.

Assign full value to distributional points and add a bonus point for a couple of 10s or for a long, hopefully solid, minor suit. If the partnership disposes of a six-card minor suit which can be readily established, game may be easy with only 22 or 23 high-card points.

As soon as you can judge that the partnership is unlikely to muster 26 points, stop as soon as possible (unless you are already in Two No Trumps). And don't venture beyond Three No Trumps when the combined hands are unlikely to contain the 33 or 34 points needed for slam.

THE OPENING BID OF ONE NO TRUMP

At cut-in bridge you will find many fashions of No Trump bidding. Without going into a technical discussion, we advise a medium No Trump of 15 to 17 points in all situations. This has the big advantage of coping with a range of hands that can be awkward to bid accurately in any other way.

When your hand falls into the appropriate range you should open One No Trump unless the hand contains a major flaw. Such features as an unguarded suit, a shortage of tenace holdings, or a biddable five-card major, are only minor flaws. Each of the following hands contains a minor flaw but should still be opened with One No Trump.

(1) ♠ 10 4   ♡ K J 6   ◇ A K J 8 5   ♣ K J 2
(2) ♠ A K 2   ♡ A 10 9 2   ◇ K Q 10   ♣ 8 4 2
(3) ♠ K 10 8 6 3   ♡ A J 4   ◇ K 4   ♣ K J 8
(4) ♠ K J 8 2   ♡ Q 10 8 6   ◇ A Q   ♣ K 10 4

The reason why it is safe to open One No Trump on the fourth hand, despite the holding of two biddable major suits, is that the technique of responses has been developed in a way that enables the partnership to reach a suit contract very easily. Holding the centre of the stage here is the Stayman response of Two Clubs.

THE STAYMAN CONVENTION

In general, a 4-4 fit in a major suit will provide a better contract than No Trumps. Over an opening bid of One No Trump responder can bid Two Clubs when he is interested in finding that sort of fit. Opener then bids a major suit if he has one, otherwise he bids Two Diamonds. Either way, the convention ends there and the subsequent bidding, if any, is natural.

This is the type of hand on which responder would bid Two Clubs in response to One No Trump:

(1) ♠ K Q 8 4   ♡ 6 5   ◇ A 10 7 2   ♣ J 10 4

If partner bids Two Spades you go to game in that suit. If he bids Two Hearts or Two Diamonds you settle for Three No Trumps. (If the opener is 4-4 in the major suits the fit in spades will not elude you, for he will bid Four Spades over Three No Trumps.)

The Stayman convention can also be used when you would prefer to play in a suit contract at the Two level.

(2) ♠ J 7 5 3   ♡ Q 6 4 2   ◇ 10 8 5 3   ♣ 4

You are more likely to achieve a plus score by bidding Two Clubs than by passing your partner's One No Trump opening. Naturally, you intend to pass any response, including Two Diamonds.

However, there are traps in this area. Responder must think ahead before using Stayman on a weak hand. On this next hand it would be inadvisable to bid Two Clubs.

(3) ♠ 4   ♡ J 7 5 3   ◇ Q 6 4 2   ♣ 10 8 6 3

The values are the same as in the previous example, but now you cannot stand a response of Two Spades. It is a close question whether to pass One No Trump or bid Two Diamonds.

OTHER RESPONSES TO ONE NO TRUMP

A raise to Two No Trumps, either direct or via Stayman, shows about 9 points. A raise to Three No Trumps shows from 10 to 15. With 16 or 17 a direct bid of Four No Trumps, not preceded by a Stayman sequence, will ask opener to bid Six No Trumps if he holds better than a minimum.

A take-out into Two of a suit is a sign-off and should *always* be respected. Nothing is more provoking than to rescue One No Trump into Two Spades on 9 x x x x and 5-4-3-1 distribution and hear partner rebid Two No Trumps, or even – perish the thought – Three No Trumps. With good support for partner's suit opener may, just, raise in competition.

A jump take-out, as in the sequence One No Trump–Three Hearts, is forcing to game and must be based on a five-card suit at least. Responder should not employ this sequence merely because he holds a five-card suit.

♠ A Q 8 4 2   ♡ A 5   ◊ 9 8 3   ♣ J 10 5

To respond Three Spades, suggesting that the hand may be better in spades than No Trumps, is a mistake. Simply raise to Three No Trumps. True, you might employ a Stayman sequence to see if partner holds four spades, but even if he does, the advantage of playing in spades is uncertain, and meanwhile you may be giving the opponents unnecessary information.

A jump in a minor suit always indicates ambitions beyond Three No Trumps, and if he is suitable for a slam the opener should cooperate.

(1) ♠ A 5 4   ♡ J 7   ◊ K J 9 6 3 2   ♣ 8 4
(2) ♠ 6 3   ♡ A 8   ◊ K 10 8 7 4 2   ♣ A K 6

On (1) simply raise One No Trump to Three No Trumps. On (2) force with Three Diamonds. A raise from partner will indicate a diamond fit and probably a ruffing value. The hand will now be worth a slam investigation. After diamonds have been bid and supported, a bid such as Five Clubs will be a slam invitation.

With a trustworthy partner the Stayman convention can be used in a quantitative sense. That is to say, you use Stayman, not in the hope of finding partner with four cards of your suit, but to provide an extra echelon of bids. In response to One No Trump you hold:

♠ K J 10 8 2   ♡ 4   ◇ A 9 8 7   ♣ 8 5 2

This hand is difficult to assess. A sign-off in Two Spades would be unenterprising, and a jump to Three Spades over-optimistic. The solution is to bid a Stayman Two Clubs and follow with Three Spades on the next round. This sequence means, conventionally, 'Three-and-a-half Spades', which is just what you would like to say here.

NO TRUMP RESPONSES TO A SUIT OPENING

After a suit opening by partner, many hands present a choice between a response in a suit and a response in No Trumps. A bid of No Trumps indicates the point count and has the advantage of not being forcing.

(*a*) *One No Trump response*. The range is 6 to 9 points. At this level there is not much freedom of choice and responder cannot wait for tenace combinations or balanced distribution. Partner opens One Spade and you hold:

(1) ♠ 6 4   ♡ A 9 5 3   ◇ K 7 4   ♣ 8 5 3 2
(2) ♠ 7   ♡ J 8 4   ◇ K 10 7 5 2   ♣ Q 7 5 3

Respond One No Trump with either hand. It would be unsound to bid Two Diamonds on the second hand, for a response at the Two level promises a minimum of 9 points, including distribution.

When partner opens in a minor suit you should generally prefer a response in a four-card major to a bid of One No Trump.

♠ K 10 7　　♡ K 9 7 3　　◇ 6 3　　♣ 8 6 4 2

In response to One Diamond, bid One Heart.

(b) *Two No Trump response*. This suggests 11 or 12 points and is one of the busiest bids in the game. A holding of 10 points is on the borderline between One No Trump and Two No Trumps. You would bid Two No Trumps only with a good ration of intermediate cards – 8s and 9s.

Scientific bidders may tell you always to show a major suit at the level of One. Listen attentively – but do not follow their advice on this type of hand:

♠ J 9 7 4　　♡ J 2　　◇ A Q 8 5　　♣ K J 6

Over One Heart, Two No Trumps is a better response than One Spade or Two Diamonds. However, if you held a similar pattern with three crisp Aces and no tenaces it would be good style to bid One Spade, even on so weak a suit as this.

A response of Two No Trumps is not recommended with a low doubleton in an unbid suit. However, one unguarded suit is not an obstacle when the alternative is to bid a suit where you have no intention of playing. In response to One Diamond, Two No Trumps is a much better move than Two Clubs on:

♠ 10 5 3　　♡ A J 4　　◇ Q 7 4　　♣ K J 9 3

If you follow an exploratory sequence on this type of hand you will still end up in No Trumps much more often than not, with the disadvantage of having pinpointed your weakness en route.

(c) *Three No Trump response*. This has a range of 13 to 15 points. It is somewhat of a grizzly bear among bids, advisable, with a good partner, only on flat 4-3-3-3 hands. Partner opens One Heart and you hold:

♠ A 5 4　　♡ Q 6　　◇ A 9 6 3　　♣ K Q 8 6

A bulldozing Three No Trumps will probably ruin any chance of reaching a delicate slam in a minor suit. The correct response is Two Clubs, but in the hurly-burly of a mixed game by all means go for the straightforward, if inelegant, Three No Trumps. In these circumstances the Bid Beautiful is all too likely to result in the Contract Horrible.

SUMMARY

Open a 15- to 17-point No Trump on balanced hands containing not more than one minor flaw.

Respond with a Stayman Two Clubs on hands that contain a major suit, a shortage, and at least 9 points. With fewer than 9 points use this convention only when you can handle any rebid by the opener.

Over a suit opening bid One No Trump on 6 to 9 points, Two No Trumps on 11 to 12, and Three No Trumps on 13 to 15.

Opening bids of Two No Trumps and Three No Trumps are discussed in Chapter Seven.

CHAPTER 4

Part Scores

The true value of a part score – Limit bids and sign-offs – Bidding to an existing part score – Summary

GOLFERS have a saying that you drive for fun but you putt for cash. The same might be said of high contracts and low contracts at bridge. In the long run you will score your fair share of games and slams; whether you win or lose will depend largely on the way you handle part-score situations.

THE TRUE VALUE OF A PART SCORE

The value of a part score is not appreciated by players who consider the points well lost if they go down 50 or 100 in a game contract which required two finesses. 'It was worth trying for game (or rubber),' they say.

'I like to *score* points' is the standard reply of one of London's most successful professionals. This is the realistic attitude, for part scores are worth much more than the figures on the score-sheet. Apart from the obvious fact that they bring the partnership nearer to game, they are the springboard from which the resourceful player achieves many fine results.

Leaving aside this psychological aspect, a part score of 40 or more has a hidden value of about 100 when not vulnerable, about 150 when vulnerable, and still more at game all. Suppose you are set one trick in a non-vulnerable contract of Four Spades. As you could have made, say, Two Spades with an overtrick, you have lost in real terms a penalty of 50, a score of 90 for tricks, plus the hidden value of 100. That is a total of 240. Had you made the game instead of being defeated, you would have gained only about 250 points as compared with playing in Two Spades and making an overtrick. The proportions when vulnerable are similar.

This explains why the best rubber-bridge players, however enterprising they may be in other phases of bidding, never press for close games. They know the value of a part score.

Still worse than missing a part score in pursuit of a close game is to climb to a precarious contract of, say, Three Spades and go one down when you could have played safely in Two. That brings us to the question of how to stop at a safe level.

LIMIT BIDS AND SIGN-OFFS

So long as there is a possibility that the partnership may hold the 26 points required for game, it is unsafe to drop the bidding. Equally, it is bad policy to go on bidding when those 26 points cannot be present in any denomination.

It follows that the trick is for one partner, as early as possible, to make a bid that defines his point count within narrow limits. The other player will then know the combined strength within a point or two. If the desired 26 points are not on the horizon the second player will pass or make a sign-off bid.

A bid that indicates the strength of a hand within about 2 points is termed a 'limit' bid, and a player who makes such a bid is said to limit his hand. The principle of limiting your hand as soon as possible lies at the heart of good bidding. Let's look at a couple of examples where failure to make a limit bid leads to a bad contract.

	West	East
♠	A Q 8 6	5 3
♡	6 5	K 9 7 4 2
♢	Q 4	A J 8 5 3
♣	A Q 10 5 3	6

The bidding goes:

West	East
1 ♣	1 ♡
1 ♠	2 ♢
2 NT	3 ♢
3 ♡	No

Not a comfortable contract, and not even a game contract. Where has the partnership gone wrong? The fault lies in East's bid of Two Diamonds. When his partner had bid both black suits there was no point in bidding diamonds unless he wanted to reach game. A simple One No Trump, limiting the hand, would have ended the auction. Here is another example:

West	East
♠ A 8 5	♠ Q 10 7 3
♡ Q J 7 6 2	♡ A 3
♢ 4	♢ K 10 8 5
♣ K Q 6 5	♣ 7 3 2

The bidding goes:

West	East
1 ♡	1 ♠
2 ♣	2 NT
3 ♠	3 NT
No	

A very dubious venture. Whose fault? Entirely that of West, who has done much too much bidding on a minimum hand. He had a chance to limit his hand on the second round by raising to Two Spades instead of introducing the clubs. This would have enabled East to drop the bidding at a fairly safe level.

These examples show two ways of limiting the hand: by bidding No Trumps or by raising partner. A rebid of one's own suit is also a limit bid unless there is already a forcing situation. A change of suit, on the other hand, is a non-limit bid with a wide range. It should be selected only when a limiting bid would be too weak. We give a few more examples now of limit bids followed by a pass or a sign-off.

Partner has limited his hand in No Trumps. We have already dealt in Chapter Three with the technique of responding to an opening bid of One No Trump.

When a bid of One No Trump is made at a later stage of the auction, the partner may either pass or sign off in a suit at the level of Two.

(1)	West	East
	1 ◇	1 ♠
	1 NT	?

Opener is marked with less than the 15 points on which he could have opened with a bid of One No Trump. At this point either Two Diamonds or Two Spades is comparatively weak, and a new suit at the Two level would not be forcing.

(2)	West	East
	1 ♠	1 NT
	?	

East has made a limit bid showing 6 to 9 points. Holding less than 17 points, opener may either pass or sign off in Two Spades. Other bids at the Two level would be less limited, but also non-forcing.

When the bidding has reached Two No Trumps a player can sign off only by rebidding his own suit.

(3)	West	East
	1 ♣	1 ♡
	2 NT	?

The rebid of Two No Trumps suggests a hand too strong for an opening One No Trump. The range is from a good 17 to a barren 19. With less than 7 points East can pass or sign off in Three Hearts. A return to partner's suit over Two No Trumps is forcing.

Partner has limited his hand by raising your suit. When partner supports your suit he will normally bid the full value of his hand. If you yourself hold a minimum for the bid you have already made, you should pass: you do not even need to compute the combined points.

West   East
1 ♠   2 ♣
3 ♣

East holds: ♠ 8 3   ♡ A 10 7 4   ◇ 7 6   ♣ K J 9 6 2

As East has already shown a minimum of 9 points by his response at the level of Two, he has nothing in reserve and should pass.

Partner has limited his hand by rebidding his suit. A simple rebid by opener in his own suit indicates a minimum opening of about 13 to 15, possibly a barren 16. To bid Two No Trumps at this point responder needs about 11 points, just as for a direct Two No Trumps. There is no sign-off other than a pass.

West   East
1 ♡   1 ♠
2 ♡   ?

East holds: ♠ A 10 7 6 5 2   ♡ 4   ◇ K 8 3   ♣ 9 5 2

A simple rebid of Two Spades would be mildly encouraging. As there are no prospects of game, East should pass.

To sum up, the way to stop in safe part scores is for one player to limit his hand as early as possible and for his partner to gauge whether there is a possibility of 26 points in any likely denomination. When this seems unlikely, he should either pass or sign off, usually in one of the suits already bid.

BIDDING TO AN EXISTING PART SCORE

How do you adjust your bidding when you have a part score? Much of the advantage will be lost if you are not well versed in the special tactics that belong to this situation.

The great difference from opening at a love score is that you need not consider your rebid. If your partner's response is enough for game you can pass. It is common, therefore, to open on some hands that would normally be passed for lack of a sound rebid. It is also common to open with a different bid from the one you would have made had there been no part score. With both sides vulnerable you hold:

♠ A Q 7 3   ♡ A Q 8   ♢ 8 5 2   ♣ 10 9 7

A player with little grasp of part-score tactics would say to himself: 'No use opening on a weak hand like this – the opponents are sure to contest and I will never be able to speak again.'

A good rubber-bridge player will take the opposite view and open One Spade. This may make it difficult for the opponents to enter, as their strength may be divided. Even if they do bid, nothing is necessarily lost. On the contrary, the opener has shown at a safe level that he holds some values and this may enable partner to contest the bidding. That is the key point: the *safest* time to bid on a moderate balanced hand is as opening bidder.

In all tense situations an opening One No Trump is an excellent move because it is so dangerous to overcall. When your side has a part score of 60 you should open One No Trump on anything from 13 points to 18, and partner should be ready for that. Also when the opponents have the part score you should open One No Trump on all borderline hands.

Pre-emptive bids at the Three and Four level are greatly influenced by the presence of a part score. With 40 below you hold:

♠ 7   ♡ 10 4   ♢ A K J 10 6 2   ♣ A 8 7 6

Normally you would open with One Diamond, because you are much too strong for Three Diamonds. If this bid is enough for game the objection disappears. Apart from the possibility that you may steal the contract, the opponents may become too 'busy' and run into a penalty double.

The spade suit is very important in part-score bidding. **In** third and fourth hand, particularly, the major-suit holdings are the deciding factor on borderline hands. Consider these two holdings:

(1) ♠ Q 5   ♡ J 7 2   ♢ A Q 8 5 3   ♣ K 5 4
(2) ♠ K Q 10   ♡ 10 9 7 3   ♢ A Q 7 6 3   ♣ 4

On (1) it will be wise to pass, for opponents will probably be able to contest in one of the majors. On (2) you have some defence against the majors and may reasonably open One Diamond.

The same sort of considerations enter when partner has opened and you hold a moderate hand in response. Partner opens One Club, the next player passes and you hold:

♠ J 4   ♡ K 9 7 3   ♢ Q 10 6 3   ♣ 8 5 2

At a love score you would respond One Diamond. In any part-score situation it is better to respond One No Trump. It is possible that you may deprive your side of a heart contract, but meanwhile you make it more difficult for the opponents to enter in spades. With a weak hand always look for the mildly pre-emptive bid.

One further problem is how to bid strong hands when you have a part score. This is admittedly tricky. Best is to express the value of your hand (or rather, *nearly* the full value, keeping a couple of points in reserve) with a natural bid even when this carries you beyond game. At 60 up, partner opens One Diamond and you hold:

♠ K J 5   ♡ A J 7   ♢ Q 5 4   ♣ K 10 9 3

Respond Two No Trumps. In the same way, One Spade–Three Spades from a part score is encouraging but not forcing.

A jump take-out, One Spade–Three Diamonds, is unconditionally forcing for one round and responder can maintain the force by changing the suit on the next round.

Opening Two bids retain their normal sense but the standard can be slightly lowered. Suppose you have 40 below and you pick up:

♠ A K J 7 5 2   ♡ 4   ◇ A Q J 6   ♣ Q 6

Open Two Spades. Partner will read this as strong but he is not obliged to respond, and if he does you should be safe in Three Spades.

Two Clubs retains its quality as a very strong hand, but Two Clubs–Two Diamonds–Two Hearts, when Two Hearts is enough for game, can be passed if responder is very weak.

SUMMARY

When a limit bid in No Trumps or in one of the partnership suits will express your hand accurately, prefer this to a nebulous change of suit.

When your partner has made a limit bid, consider whether the combined hands are likely to dispose of 26 points in any likely denomination. If not, drop the bidding in the safest part score.

When either side has a part score, incline towards the bid that will be difficult to overcall. Vary both your No Trump and your pre-emptive openings.

CHAPTER 5

The Game Zone

Overbids and underbids – The trial bid – The jump shift – Choosing between No Trumps and a suit – Choosing between two trump suits – Summary

As we have already noted, the mathematics of game bidding are a little deceptive. If you can notch the second game of a rubber you enter at least 100 below and 700 above, whereas if you make a part score you enter perhaps 60 below and 30 above. These figures much exaggerate the difference between game and part score, and the fact is that you don't want to be in games where you stand much less than an even chance of success.

If you bid game only when you hold at least 26 points you will almost always have a fair play for the contract. The only exceptions will be when the hands are misfits or there is severe duplication. But you will also find that you miss out on quite a few hands which offer a fair play for game on less than 26 points. There are the hands that fit particularly well. Sometimes you will find that you make enough tricks for game with only 22 or 23 points in the combined hands, but you needn't reproach yourself for missing those games. In the present imperfect state of the world they are more or less unbiddable. Similarly, if you reach game with 28 points and find you can't make it, you are entitled to put it down as 'one of those things'. That still leaves a considerable area, from 24 to 27, where there is room for discrimination. If you spot an exceptionally good fit you will want to be in game on 24 or 25 points. If you sense a bad fit you want to stay out of game on 26 or 27. How to diagnose such hands is our main subject in this chapter.

OVERBIDS AND UNDERBIDS

It is not always possible to express a hand with complete accuracy. Sometimes you will have to choose between a slight overbid or a slight underbid. When this dilemma also involves a choice between game and part score, there is a very useful test which not many players think about.

If you are in a safe part-score contract you should under-bid and not jeopardize that score. If the part-score contract is no certainty you should be more willing to overbid to reach game.

Of course, we are not saying anything so silly as that if you are not sure whether you can make Two Spades you might as well bid Four. If you compare the next two examples you will see what we mean.

Opener	Responder
1 ♣	1 ♡
1 NT	?

Responder holds: ♠ Q 4 ♡ K J 6 3 2 ◇ A 8 5 ♣ 7 6 3

The opener's range is between 13 and $14\frac{1}{2}$ and responder has 11, counting distribution. Game is possible if opener has a maximum. On the other hand, if opener is minimum even Two No Trumps may fail. Responder should therefore be content to play in the safe contract of One No Trump.

In the next example the same test points to a calculated overbid.

Opener	Responder
1 ◇	2 NT
?	

Opener holds: ♠ A 2 ♡ 8 3 ◇ K 10 8 7 6 4 ♣ A 9 5

Responder's bid of Two No Trumps suggests from $10\frac{1}{2}$ to 12 points. As the opener has only 13, counting 2 points for the long diamonds, it may seem on the surface that he should pass. However, that would be unintelligent, for if declarer can bring in the diamonds he will probably make game, and if he can't he may not make Two No Trumps. A conservative sign-off of Three Diamonds would not be wrong, but we would be prepared to gamble and bid Three No Trumps.

Another not-so-obvious consideration may favour an underbid in preference to a raise to game. Suppose you open One Heart and your partner responds Two Diamonds, suggesting a minimum of 9 points. You hold:

♠ A 3   ♡ A K 7 5 4   ◇ 6 4 2   ♣ K Q 4

With 17 points, counting 1 for the long hearts, you are theoretically worth a game bid, presumably Three No Trumps. However, you cannot be sure that No Trumps will be the right spot. There may be a weakness in spades, for example. It is better to hold back a little with Two No Trumps, allowing room for partner to bid at the Three level. The principle is worth remembering: *prefer a slight underbid to an overbid when this will keep open a wider choice of contracts.* Another example:

Opener	Responder
1 ♡	2 ◇
?	

Opener holds: ♠ 7 6 2   ♡ A K Q 4   ◇ A Q J 6   ♣ J 2

With 17 points in high cards the opener should normally look for a strength-showing rebid, which in this case could only be a jump to Four Diamonds. However, there will probably be duplication in the red suits, and with so many losers in the black suits the only game may be in No Trumps. Opener should underbid a little with Three Diamonds, leaving room for Three No Trumps.

When it seems close whether you should bid game or not, it is common-sense to invite partner's cooperation in making the decision. That brings us to an important manoeuvre, the trial bid.

When a suit – particularly a major suit – has been agreed by a raise, the bid of a new suit is temporarily forcing and invites the responder to bid game if he has anything in reserve.

Opener	Responder
1 ♡	2 ♡
3 ♣	

The trial bid of Three Clubs asks responder to bid game if he is above average in terms of points or if he is only average but has a fit in the trial suit. A doubleton honour, such as K x or Q x, always constitutes a good fit; so does a singleton when accompanied by good trump support. A typical hand for the opener in the above sequence would be:

♠ A 7   ♡ K Q 10 8 5   ◇ A 2   ♣ Q 9 5 3

After One Heart–Two Hearts much will depend on responder's holding in clubs. That is precisely the message conveyed by a trial bid of Three Clubs.

<u>A new suit after a raise in a minor is also forcing.</u> It may be a trial bid on a holding such as A x x or the suit may be genuine.

Opener	Responder
1 ♣	1 ◇
2 ◇	2 ♡

Here Two Hearts may be looking towards Three No Trumps or it may denote a heart suit; in any case it is forcing.

A trial bid admittedly gives information to the opponents as well as to partner. But there is no law against sending forth an occasional smokescreen. On this next hand your opening bid of One Spade is raised to Two.

♠ A K J 8 2   ♡ A Q 9 3   ◇ A   ♣ 5 3 2

You do not need to make a genuine trial bid, as you intend to bid game in spades. However, it may be a good idea to bid Three Clubs en route. This may divert the opposition from a club attack.

In general, a trial bid after a major suit has been raised is slightly more encouraging than Three of the suit. After One Heart–Two Hearts, Two No Trumps suggests a balanced hand of about 17 points. Unlike a trial bid, it is not forcing.

THE JUMP SHIFT

So far we have been considering how to make borderline decisions in the game zone. Another problem is to make certain that your side does not stop short of game when you can see that the values are present. A trial bid is forcing for one round, as we have seen, and in most cases a new suit at the level of Three is forcing. When one of these bids is not available it may be necessary to jump in a new suit. This is called a jump shift and is unconditionally forcing to game on both partners. Partner opens One Club and you hold:

♠ A Q 7   ♡ K Q J 5 3   ◊ 10 2   ♣ K 5 4

Force with Two Hearts. It is true that One Heart would be forcing for the moment, but it is bad economy to make the low bid now and be forced to jump later. Once you have forced with Two Hearts the bidding can develop at leisure, for neither player is allowed to drop the bidding short of game. A total of 16 points, including distribution, is about the minimum for a jump shift (or 'force', as it is usually called). Naturally, the fit with partner is an important consideration. You hold:

♠ 5   ♡ A 10 6   ◊ K Q 8 4   ♣ A Q 7 5 2

Over One Heart you are strong enough to force with Three Clubs, but over One Spade it would be better to approach more gradually with Two Clubs. Of course, you intend to reach game eventually; on the next round you can keep the pot boiling with Three Diamonds.

The jump shift can also be employed by either player at a later stage of the auction. You open One Club, partner bids One Diamond, and you hold:

♠ A Q J 7 2   ♡ 6   ♢ K 7   ♣ A K J 5 3

With 20 points and a mild fit for partner you certainly intend to reach game. Force with Two Spades and on the next round repeat the spades to show you are 5-5 or 5-6 in the black suits.

CHOOSING BETWEEN NO TRUMPS AND A SUIT

When you have decided you want to be in game you may still have to choose between playing in a suit or in No Trumps. There is something of a paradox here, for it does not follow that the stronger the suit the more you should be inclined to play in a trump contract.

West	East
1 ♢	1 ♠
2 ♣	3 ♠
?	

As West, the less you have in partner's suit the less you should be inclined to attempt Three No Trumps. Suppose you hold:

♠ 5   ♡ A 8 7   ♢ A J 8 4 3   ♣ K Q 5 3

If you have reasonable trust in your partner's bidding and play you should bid Four Spades. Next best is a pass. You should definitely not bid game in No Trumps because, with a singleton spade, you may well have neither time nor entries to establish dummy's long suit. If you held a similar count, but with K x or Q x in spades, you could reasonably expect to harvest the spade suit. Now Three No Trumps could well be the right contract.

Decisions of that sort are responsible for a big turnover. A similar problem arises after this sequence:

Opener	Responder
1 ◇	1 ♡
2 NT	3 ♡
?	

Opener holds: ♠ K Q 4   ♡ 7 5   ◇ A Q J 6 2   ♣ A J 3

West's Two No Trump rebid has indicated 17 to 19 points and he actually holds 18, counting 1 point for the fifth diamond. North's bid of Three Hearts means 'Despite your strong rebid I doubt whether we can make game in No Trumps or in hearts'. On the present hand South should pass. Strengthen it a little, but still with the same holding in hearts, and it will be far better to raise the hearts than bid Three No Trumps.

Suppose next that after the same bidding opener holds:

♠ K 6 4   ♡ A Q 3   ◇ A Q 8 6   ♣ K 9 4

Now he can be almost sure of being able to run the heart suit. He should bid Three No Trumps, not fancying the idea of a lead through one of his Kings in Four Hearts.

A trump suit divided more equally between the two hands is a different proposition. With 4-4, in particular, it will be possible to increase the trick-winning power of the trump suit by ruffing in one hand while retaining intact the trump length in the other. When a 4-4 fit has been found in a major suit it will seldom be wise to look for any other contract.

♠ K 10 4   ♡ A J 8 5   ◇ K Q 7 3   ♣ K Q

As you are over strength for One No Trump you open One Heart and partner raises to Three Hearts. Now it would be a mistake to rebid Three No Trumps on the grounds that you are fairly balanced and the hearts are not strong. You should assume that playing in hearts with a 4-4 fit will be worth at least one extra trick. You will also be protected against the run of a long suit by the defenders.

CHOOSING BETWEEN TWO TRUMP SUITS

Many bidding sequences lead to the same crunch question:
whether to play in your suit or partner's. The question arises
on the following hand.

Opener	Responder
1 ♡	1 ♠
3 ♡	3 ♠
?	

Opener holds: ♠ 5 3 ♡ A K Q 9 6 2 ◇ A 6 4 ♣ K 9

Opener has three possible calls – Four Hearts, Four
Spades, and Three No Trumps. As the hearts may not be
solid, Three No Trumps, with only one stop in each minor,
is unsound. As between Four Hearts and Four Spades,
<u>follow the principle of playing in the trump suit of the
weaker hand.</u> Your hand is sure to be useful to the declarer
in spades; you cannot be sure that his hand will be worth
much in hearts.

Here is a rather more delicate example:

Opener	Responder
1 ♡	1 ♠
2 NT	3 ♡
?	

Opener holds: ♠ 5 3 2 ♡ A 9 8 7 2 ◇ A Q 6 ♣ A K

Four Hearts may seem obvious, but Three Spades, giving
partner a chance to play the hand if he has five spades, is
better. As before, the strong hand may gain little support
from the weak hand, playing in hearts. With spades as
trumps the strong hand will be a very suitable dummy.

Another small surprise: when you have two suits, both
divided 5-3, you should aim to play in the weaker of those
combinations. You hold this hand:

♠ J 10 6 3 2   ♡ A K Q 7 5   ◇ A K   ♣ 4

You open One Spade and responder bids One No Trump.
You force with Three Hearts and partner bids Three Spades.

It is quite likely that partner holds three cards in each major and many players would make one more attempt to play in hearts, bidding Four Hearts. This would be a great mistake. If you don't believe it, just look at these two hands in combination:

West	East
♠ J 10 6 3 2	♠ 8 5 4
♡ A K Q 7 5	♡ 6 3 2
◇ A K	◇ J 8 5
♣ 4	♣ A J 6 5

Which contract would you prefer to be in – Four Spades or Four Hearts? Try Four Spades first. A club is led, you win with the Ace and lead trumps. You ruff the club return and lead a second trump. If the opponents win and fire back a third club you ruff and set about the hearts, leaving the enemy with only the master trump to win. You easily make the contract if both major suits are 3-2 – and you might well be able to cope with a 4-1 break in hearts.

What happens in Four Hearts? You win the club opening and play a spade, a slightly better move than drawing trumps. You ruff the club return and lead another spade. Another club reduces you to ♡ A K Q and there is still a spade winner against you. Prospects are poor.

It follows from this example that when partner is expected to hold equal length in two suits and you hold K x of one, x x of the other, you should prefer to play in the suit where you hold x x. The slogan is: *Strong suits make good side suits. Weak suits, if long enough, make good trump suits.*

SUMMARY

When game is borderline, don't disturb a safe part score.

When a suit has been agreed by a raise, any new suit is a trial bid, forcing for one round.

As responder, you need upwards of 16 points for a jump shift. As opener, force (or bid game) when you can count 26 points in the combined hands.

Don't attempt a doubtful Three No Trumps when you are weak in partner's long suit.

As between trump suits of equal length, aim to play in the weaker of the two. In general, prefer to play in the trump suit of the weaker hand.

CHAPTER 6

Slam Bidding

Slam valuation – The Blackwood convention – Cue bids – Summary

A GOOD record in slam bidding is rare, even for experts. Some players would be better off if they resolved never to bid a slam in any circumstances. Quite a lot more would profit if they bid slams less frequently than they do.

These are observable facts. It is also an observable fact that no genuine bridge player has the slightest intention of cutting down on his slam bidding. Recognizing this, we offer a three-point plan to slash slam losses:

(1) Realize that accurate valuation – gauging whether you have twelve playing tricks – is far more important than finding out how many Aces your partner holds.

(2) Treat the Blackwood convention as merely a final check-up – a means of staying out of a slam when you are short of two Aces.

(3) Cultivate the art of cue-bidding, which has the advantage of improving your estimate of slam chances while at the same time helping to locate controls.

SLAM VALUATION

The first item on the agenda is to establish that your hands belong in the slam zone – that you can amass twelve tricks unless there are two quick losers. The majority of slam failures occur when players put the cart before the horse, inquiring for Aces before they know whether enough playing tricks are there.

How can you tell you are in the slam zone? Point count

will take you a long way. You will find that 33 points in the combined hands will usually be sufficient to give you an even chance for a slam, and that, mathematically, is what you want. Take the simplest case. Your partner opens One No Trump and you hold:

♠ K Q 7 ♡ A J 5 ◇ K Q J 3 ♣ Q 10 7

As there must be a minimum of 33 points in the two hands you can go straight to Six No Trumps. It is true that you could just be missing the Ace and King of clubs. That would be extremely unlucky. In practice it is better to accept that risk rather than attempt to explore your partner's club holding.

When your combined count of 33 points includes distributional points, then it is much more necessary to check on controls. The bidding begins:

Opener	Responder
1 ♠	4 ♠
?	

Opener holds: ♠ K Q 8 4 2 ♡ 6 ◇ A K Q 7 ♣ K Q 5

Responder has indicated 13 to 15 points, so the values for a slam are certainly present. As it is possible that two Aces are missing, opener should bid a Blackwood Four No Trumps, as described later.

Here the bidding is a little more complicated, but the conclusion is the same: the playing tricks are there but it is necessary to check on controls.

Opener	Responder
1 ♣	2 ♡
3 ♣	3 NT
?	

Opener holds: ♠ K J 4 ♡ J 3 ◇ J 7 ♣ A K Q 8 4 2

To force on a balanced hand responder should hold upwards of 16 points. Counting 2 points for the long clubs,

opener can underwrite a total of 33, so is willing to reach
Six No Trumps – likely to be better than Six Clubs, as the
responder may have tenace holdings. However, although
the values are surely there, the partnership may hold only
30 or 31 high-card points and the chance of losing two fast
tricks should not be disregarded. Therefore opener should
bid Four Clubs, hoping that partner will show controls.

In the slam zone as in the game zone, you cannot be a
really good bidder unless you are able to make allowances
for 'fit' – or the lack of it. Consider this sequence:

Opener	Responder
1 ♠	2 ♡
4 ♡	?

Responder holds: ♠ 8 3 2   ♡ A Q J 5 4   ◇ K 4   ♣ K J 6

Responder holds 15 points and so far has promised only 9.
The opener ought to hold about 16 to 18 for his raise to Four
Hearts. If opener is maximum the combined count will be
fully 33. Should responder therefore try for slam?

Certainly many players would initiate Blackwood on the
responding hand, but in the long run that must be wrong.
Responder should look at it this way: 'As opener is long in
both major suits he will be short in one of the minor suits,
possibly in both. At least one of my Kings will be opposite a
singleton and so wasted. Another unattractive feature is the
holding of three low cards in partner's spade suit. As the
hands cannot be a good fit, and as we will hold 33 points
only if partner is maximum, I will not embark on any slam
try.'

Prospects would be quite different if responder held the
same number of points, distributed like this:

♠ Q 10   ♡ A J 9 5 4   ◇ A 4   ♣ K 8 3 2

Now the hands appear to fit well and so long as opener
holds an Ace there will surely be a good play for the slam.
The next step with this hand would be a Blackwood Four
No Trumps.

You will encounter many hands where the diagnosis is less clear-cut than in the examples above. Our advice? When in doubt, and unable to resolve the doubt at a safe level, be content with a game.

THE BLACKWOOD CONVENTION

If you have been watching for this with the impatience of a lover awaiting his betrothed, the chances are that you are one of the many who use the convention too freely. No doubt you know how it works: over Four No Trumps the responder bids Five Clubs with no Ace (or with four), Five Diamonds with one Ace, Five Hearts with two Aces, and Five Spades with three. If interested in a grand slam, the Blackwoodite may then bid Five No Trumps to ask for Kings according to the same schedule.

The time to use Blackwood is when three conditions are met:

(1) It must be evident that there are enough playing tricks for slam.

(2) There must be no danger (when a minor suit is involved) that an unfavourable response may take the partnership beyond a safe level.

(3) The situation must be such that it will suffice to know *how many* Aces partner holds, rather than which ones.

A large slice of the nation's bridge players are unimpressed by the cogency of this last proposition. They gaily use Blackwood in a situation like this:

Opener	*Responder*
1 ♠	3 ♣
3 ♡	3 ♠
4 ♣	4 NT (?)

Responder holds: ♠ K J 9 3   ♡ K 4   ◇ Q J 6   ♣ A K J 5

Opener loyally admits possession of two Aces – and responder is still at sea! Perhaps there are two losing diamonds, perhaps not. The intelligent action here is to bid Five Hearts over Four Spades, making it clear that the only worry concerns the unbid suit.

Because the answer to Blackwood only tells 'how many', it is generally wrong to use the convention (a) with a void, and (b) when, as in the example above, the response may leave you uncertain whether there are two losers in a particular suit.

Here is a situation where it is right to use Blackwood:

Opener	Responder
1 ♡	2 ◇
2 ♠	2 NT
4 ◇	?

Responder holds: ♠ K 6   ♡ 7   ◇ A 9 8 6 4 3   ♣ J 10 7 2

The opener has bid three suits, making it clear that he is short in the unbid club suit. As the hands appear to fit perfectly, slam is almost certain if the opener holds two Aces. If (most unlikely on this bidding) opener has only one Ace, the partnership will be safe in Five Diamonds.

Players frequently break the first condition mentioned above – that there should be an assurance of sufficient playing tricks before Blackwood is launched. This sequence, or its close relative, can be observed in almost every session:

Opener	Responder
1 ♡	1 ♠
3 ♣	3 ♠
4 NT (?)	

Opener holds: ♠ K 8 3   ♡ A Q 7 4   ◇ K J   ♣ A K 8 5

Here the opener is inclined to think: 'Now that spades have been rebid my hand looks strong enough for slam. If partner holds two Aces we can hardly fail. If he has only one I am still going to take a chance.'

The mistake here is partly one of valuation, partly of

method. Opener has already shown the full power of his
hand by forcing to game with the jump rebid of Three Clubs.
Responder may hold no more than 6 or 7 points, and in that
case even a contract at the Five level will be precarious. All
the opener is worth now is Four Spades. In any case, Four
No Trumps would be the wrong way to proceed, for the
information that partner holds one Ace will not settle
whether slam is there.

Finally, a Blackwood bid is particularly injudicious when
the response to Four No Trumps may carry the partnership
beyond a safe level. That folly occurs in the following
auction:

Opener	Responder
1 ♣	1 ◊
3 ◊	4 NT (?)

Responder holds: ♠ K 10 8 3   ♡ 4   ◊ K Q 10 8 5 3   ♣ J 4

Responder thinks: 'This must be a slam if partner has got
three Aces. I'll bid Four No Trumps to find out.' Very naïve,
for opener may bid Five Hearts, showing only two Aces, and
now the partnership is overboard. The best action in this
example is to bid Three Spades, giving partner a chance to
launch Blackwood if he wants to. Alternatively, a jump to
Five Diamonds would probably inspire partner to bid Six if
he held three Aces.

Still another hazard lies in wait for the incorrigible Blackwoodite: in some sequences partner may construe a bid of
Four No Trumps as natural, not conventional. Even experts
– nay, especially experts – have been known to have costly
misunderstandings about this. It is wise to establish two
agreements:

(1) Four No Trumps is always natural if neither player
has bid a suit genuinely (for example, if they have bid only
No Trumps, plus a Stayman Two Clubs and Two Diamonds).

(2) Four No Trumps is also natural when, although suits
have been called, it is clear that neither player has settled on
one of them as a trump suit.

Applying this last principle, how would you regard **Four No Trumps** in the following sequences?

(1)	Opener	Responder
	1 ♠	2 ♡
	3 NT	4 NT

Natural, because no trump suit has been agreed by the partnership, either by a raise or by implication. In technical terms, responder is giving a quantitative raise of No Trumps. (If responder wants to know about Aces in this kind of situation he must bid a minor suit over Three No Trumps and on the next round bid Four No Trumps.)

(2)	Opener	Responder
	1 ♠	2 ♡
	4 NT	

Conventional, for it would make no sense to jump to Four No Trumps merely to show a hand too strong for a bid of Three No Trumps. Clearly the opener holds a big fit in hearts and is headed for slam in that suit.

(3)	Opener	Responder
	1 ♣	1 ♢
	3 NT	4 ♢
	4 NT	

Natural – and a distinct sign-off to boot. Responder must be allowed to bid Four Diamonds in this sort of sequence to say, 'If your hand is suitable for play in diamonds, there may be a slam.' It follows that opener must be allowed to bid Four No Trumps as a sign-off on an unsuitable hand.

CUE BIDS

As our description of Blackwood has been tempered by numerous warnings, what action do we recommend when there is some objection to the use of the convention? The answer on the great majority of hands is a cue bid.

When a trump suit has been agreed and the partnership is committed to game, any bid in a side suit is a cue bid. It shows control in that suit, usually the Ace or void, but sometimes a King or singleton. It also indicates that the player has reserves of strength. The degree of encouragement conveyed by a cue bid depends largely on whether it takes the bidding beyond game level.

Opener	*Responder*
1 ♣	1 ♠
3 ♣	4 ◊

Responder may be very strong, intending to go to Six in any event, but for the moment his Four Diamond bid says: 'Having heard your raise to Three Spades I think a slam is possible. I have first-round control of diamonds. If your hand is suitable for slam, please make some encouraging noise.'

At this point the opener would sign off in Four Spades if his raise was based mainly on distribution. With a fair share of 'tops' he might respond with a cue bid in hearts or clubs. A cue bid of Four Hearts would not be much more than an admission that a heart control was held; but Five Clubs, taking the partnership beyond game, would obviously be a more positive acceptance of the slam try.

In the next example several cue bids are made and as the auction develops each player gets a clear picture of his partner's hand.

West	*East*
♠ 6	♠ J 7 4
♡ A K 8 7 2	♡ Q 10 6 5
◊ K 9 4	◊ A 8 3 2
♣ A Q J 3	♣ K 7

The bidding goes:

West	East
1 ♥	3 ♥
4 ♣[1]	4 ♦[2]
4 ♠[3]	5 ♣[4]
6 ♥[5]	Pass

[1] The first cue bid, not taking the partnership beyond game. If this was met by a sign-off of Four Hearts, West would not persevere.

[2] East shows a control in diamonds – probably the Ace. As his hand is limited by the raise to Three Hearts, East is fully entitled to accept the slam suggestion.

[3] This bid of Four Spades takes the bidding beyond game and is therefore a positive slam try. There is a slight inference here that West holds only second-round control of spades, for with the Ace he would probably have cue-bid that suit before clubs. (The usual policy is to make the *cheapest* cue bid available.)

[4] Now that his partner has embarked on the open sea, East is quite willing to show his club control.

[5] It looks as though the hands fit very well. A favourable omen from West's point of view is that his partner has not bid spades at any stage. This suggests that little is wasted in that suit.

Barring a 4-0 break in trumps, Six Hearts is a certainty, as two diamonds in dummy can be discarded on declarer's clubs. And the two hands contain only 27 high-card points.

SUMMARY

As the first step towards a slam, gauge whether the two hands can win twelve tricks, subject to there being two quick losers.

Use Blackwood only when you want to know how many Aces partner holds, rather than which ones.

When uncertain whether the values for a slam are present, or when you need to identify specific controls, proceed by way of cue bids.

CHAPTER 7

The Big Bids

*Two Clubs is artificial – Other Two bids mean length
and strength – The Two No Trump opening – The
Three No Trump opening – Summary*

THE big bids are not high bids. They are all opening bids at
the Two level. All bids of that sort are strong, and no hand
is too strong for that sort of bid.

The purpose of a Two bid is to proclaim the character of
the hand at once so that you do not need to jump the bidding
later. You establish quickly that game values are present and
you still have time to explore for slam at a safe level.

It is rare for a player to hold game in his own hand.
Therefore it makes sense to use a single bid, Two Clubs, to
deal with the occasional rock-crusher where opener intends
to reach game with little or no support from his partner.
Other opening bids of Two of a suit are forcing for one
round and indicate a strong distributional hand.

TWO CLUBS IS ARTIFICIAL

You do not need a club suit to open Two Clubs. You do
need at least 23 points in high cards and distribution. If the
hand is balanced and the points are all in high cards, the
rebid will be Two or Three No Trumps. If the hand is unbalanced, opener will announce a suit on the second round;
responder must then keep the bidding open until game is
reached.

When responder is weak – fewer than 7 points – he gives
the negative response of Two Diamonds. Anything else is a
positive response. When his suit is clubs or diamonds he

may need to respond at the Three level. As this consumes a round of bidding it is inadvisable to bid Three Diamonds (or Three Clubs) on a borderline hand or on a four-card suit.

After the first round the subsequent auction follows natural lines. A negative response is much more frequent than a positive and we will consider that first. Suppose the opener holds a minimum balanced hand such as:

♠ A K 9 3   ♥ A Q J   ♦ K Q 4 2   ♣ K J

After Two Clubs–Two Diamonds the opener rebids Two No Trumps, showing 23 or 24 points. This sequence is not forcing: responder may pass on a worthless hand but he needs only 3 points, or Q x x x x, for a raise to game. This is the only situation where the bidding may be dropped below game after a Two Club opening.

When the opener bids a suit on the second round, creating a forcing-to-game situation, responder should strive to show any feature of his hand rather than make an uninformative bid of Two No Trumps. For example:

Opener	*Responder*
2 ♣	2 ♦
2 ♥	?

Responder holds: ♠ J 10 7 2   ♥ 10 4   ♦ Q J 6 3   ♣ 8 5 4

Two Spades is better now than Two No Trumps. As responder has already indicated a poor hand he should not be nervous of telling where his length is.

After the sequence Two Clubs–Two Diamonds–Two No Trumps, Three Clubs by the responder is Stayman type. The convention does not operate in quite the same way as the Stayman Two Clubs over One No Trump. Over Three Clubs partner is asked to bid his *lowest-ranking four-card suit*, whether major or minor. Thus Three Diamonds indicates four diamonds and Three No Trumps means that the only four-card suit is clubs. When the opener has named his lowest suit the bidding continues on the same lines until a fit is found or Three No Trumps is reached. Here is an example:

West	East
♠ A Q 8 3	♠ 6 5 2
♡ K 8	♡ Q J 10 3
◇ A Q 10 2	◇ 6 4
♣ A K J	♣ Q 8 5 2

The bidding goes:

West	East
2 ♣[1]	2 ◇[2]
2 NT[3]	3 ♣[4]
3 ◇[5]	3 ♡[6]
3 ♠[7]	3 NT[8]
Pass	

[1] Artificial and forcing.

[2] Negative response, less than 7 or 8 points.

[3] Balanced 23 or 24 count.

[4] Artificial, asking opener to bid his four-card suits 'upwards'.

[5] The lowest four-card suit.

[6] Showing four hearts.

[7] Showing four spades.

[8] A sign-off. Evidently responder was interested only in hearts as a possible alternative to Three No Trumps.

Long-winded, and on this occasion leading nowhere in particular. Nevertheless, this style of bidding is an essential plank in the technique for coping with big hands. It is also used, as we shall see later, over an opening bid of Two No Trumps.

Whenever there is a positive response to Two Clubs the combined hands must already contain a minimum of 30 points, so an eventual slam is more than likely. However, there is no need to step up the pace. If opener has the sort of hand on which he would have rebid Two No Trumps over a negative he should make the same rebid over a positive (unless he proposes to raise the suit). The responder, too, should not leap about unless he has extra values to announce.

The bidding begins:

Opener	Responder
2 ♣	2 ♠
3 ♡	?

Responder holds: ♠ A J 9 6   ♡ Q 8 5 4   ◇ J 7   ♣ 10 4 2

A slam is very likely now, but responder has little in reserve and a simple raise to Four Hearts is enough for the moment. The opener, who has heard the positive response and the raise of hearts, will almost surely continue.

A jump to Three No Trumps by the opener, over Two Diamonds or over a positive response at the Two level, suggests a balanced 25 or 26 points. Any continuation over Three No Trumps is a slam try and Four Clubs is Stayman type.

OTHER TWO BIDS MEAN LENGTH AND STRENGTH

Opening bids of Two Spades, Two Hearts and Two Diamonds are forcing for one round. They indicate strong distributional hands lacking the high-card values for an opening Two Clubs but too good for an opening bid of One.

When your hand seems on the borderline between a Two bid and an ordinary One bid, ask yourself this question: 'If I open One and partner passes, will there be a danger that we have missed a game?' The following hand is not strong enough for Two Clubs and the choice is between Two Hearts and One Heart:

♠ K 10   ♡ A K J 10 8 3   ◇ 4   ♣ A K 8 2

The short answer on this one is that if partner has three hearts and an Ace you want to be in game, so you should open Two Hearts. This commits you to the Three level only. Most hands that warrant an opening Two bid contain between 16 and 19 high-card points and at least eight playing tricks. This type of opening is called an 'Acol Two' after the popular Acol system. (As a matter of fact, most of the bidding in this book is on Acol lines.)

The negative response to an Acol Two is Two No Trumps. The requirements for a positive are higher than over Two Clubs. It is advisable to bid Two No Trumps whenever you hold less than 10 points in high cards, unless you have good support for partner or can bid a suit at the Two level; in that case, 7 or 8 points may suffice.

♠ 7 2   ♡ A Q 8 3   ◇ 6 4 2   ♣ J 9 6 4

This is just worth Two Hearts over Two Diamonds. Over Two Spades bid Two No Trumps, for quite likely your heart suit will be of little interest to the opener.

As an Acol Two is always based on one very good suit, or two good suits, you may support on Q x or x x x. However, you still need the requirements for a positive response and in some circles an immediate raise promises an Ace. With a moderate hand you bid Two No Trumps first and support the suit later. A double raise shows a fair hand with good trump support but no Ace.

One of the great virtues of the Acol Two is that it copes with strong two-suiters where there is a fit only for the second suit. This is a typical example:

West	East
♠ A 2	♠ 10 8 3
♡ A K Q 10 4	♡ 6
◇ A Q 6 3 2	◇ K 10 8 5 4
♣ 8	♣ J 7 3 2

The bidding goes:

West	East
2 ♡	2 NT
3 ◇	5 ◇
6 ◇	Pass

Clearly East would have to pass an opening One Heart. After his negative response to Two Hearts he can safely jump in diamonds. West is not tempted to think of Seven because partner is unlikely to hold the King of diamonds and the Ace of clubs.

THE TWO NO TRUMP OPENING

This shows a balanced 20 to 22 points. Responder needs about 5 points, or a suit as good as K x x x x, for a raise to game. A five-card suit headed by the Ace or King is a distinctly better holding than 9 x x x x with an Ace outside.

Any response to a Two No Trump opening is forcing to game in effect. A simple take-out into Three of a suit may be weak or may be the prelude to slam investigation. It is unnecessary, therefore, to make a jump response on a good hand. On the contrary, a jump to Four Hearts or Four Spades over Two No Trumps is a 'stop' bid.

We have already described how the conventional bid of Three Clubs can be used after a sequence beginning Two Clubs–Two Diamonds–Two No Trumps. The same Three Club bid works in exactly the same way when the opening bid is Two No Trumps. As this is the standard way to locate a 4-4 fit, it follows that a direct Three Diamonds, Three Hearts or Three Spades over Two No Trumps shows a five-card suit.

Responder should not employ the Three Club bid when he holds a useful five-card major. The following example illustrates a very common error:

	West	*East*
♠	A K Q	♠ J 7 6
♡	Q J 7	♡ K 10 8 3 2
◇	A 10 5 4 3	◇ K 8 2
♣	A 10	♣ 8 4

The bidding goes:

West	*East*
2 NT	3 ♣ (?)
3 ◇	3 ♡
3 NT	?

East misguidedly bids a conventional Three Clubs and West dutifully shows a diamond suit. When East bids Three Hearts the opener, placing him with four hearts only, bids Three No Trumps, denying four cards in hearts or spades. Now East is stranded. As his partner may hold only a doubleton heart, and Three No Trumps may be lay-down, he probably leaves him to play in this horrendous contract.

Suppose East had made the correct bid of Three Hearts on the first round. Then West, with a suitable hand for a slam in hearts, would make some encouraging noise like Three Spades or Four Clubs. As East has no ambitions beyond game he signs off in Four Hearts, ending the auction.

THE THREE NO TRUMP OPENING

The way to bid a very strong balanced hand, as we have seen, is to open Two Clubs and rebid Two No Trumps or Three No Trumps. Thus a different meaning attaches to an opening bid of Three No Trumps. Conventionally, this shows a solid minor suit, usually of seven cards, and little or nothing outside. From then on, partner is in complete command. If the bid is doubled, it will be up to him to decide whether to take to the hills.

With a hand on which Three No Trumps will obviously be unmakable responder may either pass, in the hope of daunting the foe, or take out into Four of the opener's minor. (If he cannot tell from his own hand which is the long suit, he bids Four Clubs.) Suppose he holds a better hand such as:

♠ 10   ♡ A K 8 2   ◇ K J 7 3 2   ♣ 8 6 4

Over Three No Trumps the correct response is Five Clubs!

SUMMARY

Open Two Clubs with 23 points, forcing to game except for the rebid of Two No Trumps.

Open an Acol Two bid with 16 to 19 points and strong

distribution. Any positive response promises upwards of 8 points. A direct raise to Three should include an Ace.

Open Two No Trumps on 20–22. Over Two No Trumps (or Two Clubs–Two Diamonds–Two No Trumps) Three Clubs asks for four-card suits 'upwards'.

Open Three No Trumps with a solid minor suit and at most one Queen outside.

CHAPTER 8

Pre-emptive Bids

The 500 mark – Opening with a Three bid – Responding to a Three bid – Later tactics – Other pre-emptive bids – How to counter an opposing pre-empt – Summary

A DICTIONARY definition of 'pre-empt' is 'to secure as first-comer'. Every opening at the level of Three or higher is based on that idea. Opener is warning his partner that his hand is playable only in the suit he calls. He is also trying to shut the opponents out.

A Three bid is invariably weaker in high cards than a bid of One. The player who opens with a Three bid takes the view that opponents could make better use of bidding space than he can, so he sets out to deprive them of space.

Of course, you need a quota of playing tricks. Opponents know what you are doing and will often double rather than allow themselves to be shut out or hustled into the wrong contract. When you pre-empt you must budget for that.

THE 500 MARK

It is no disgrace to go down 500 points so long as you save a game. It is no great bargain, either. With neither side vulnerable the transaction shows a slight loss, with both sides vulnerable a slight gain. On the whole, it is a fair trade. When you pre-empt you must have this figure very much in mind.

It follows that not vulnerable you may pre-empt at the Three level on any hand that is likely to produce six tricks even if partner has no support. A suit like K Q J x x x x, with little or nothing outside, represents a typical Three bid.

Vulnerable, you need to be within two tricks of your contract to hold the penalty to 500. Thus a hand worth a vulnerable Three bid will be closer to a Four bid not vulnerable.

Even if you follow these standards scrupulously you will go down more than 500 when the trump suit is stacked against you. Worse, you will sometimes concede a penalty when there is no game for the opposition. Against that, your pre-empt will often cause the opponents to land in the wrong contract. When that happens, even if you register only 100 on the score-sheet, your pre-empt will in reality have gained much more.

OPENING WITH A THREE BID

When you are considering a pre-empt of any kind, position at the table is of great importance. In first or second hand it is dangerous to stray far beyond the limits of six or seven playing tricks and a maximum of about 9 points in high cards. If you elect to open Three Hearts on A K J x x x with a King outside, there is a grave danger that partner, holding enough for an easy game, will pass, expecting you to be much weaker.

In general, too, it is unwise to pre-empt in first or second position when your hand is well playable in another suit, especially a major suit.

♠ Q J 7 5   ♡ 4   ◇ K Q J 8 4 2   ♣ 9 3

Do not open Three Diamonds on this type of hand. Such a bid may prevent your side from bidding spades, either as a sacrifice over Four Hearts or as a genuine game. Partner will not introduce a moderate suit over a Three bid.

Three bids after partner has passed are a different proposition altogether. For one thing, it may now be right to open with more than the regulation number of high-card points.

Suppose opponents are vulnerable and after two passes you hold:

♠ A 4   ♡ 7   ◇ J 8 5 3   ♣ A Q J 8 6 2

It is possible, but not likely, that there is a game your way. Forget about that and open Three Clubs. Partner will place you with a weaker hand, but this is a virtuous confidence trick: you may hold the contract and just make it or you may tempt the opponents into an indiscretion. In fourth position, also, we would try to snatch the part score with a bid of Three Clubs.

Similarly, when partner has passed you may choose to ignore the advice to pre-empt only on one-suited hands. Say that you hold:

♠ Q 10 8 4   ♡ –   ◇ A J 9 8 6 3 2   ♣ 5 4

In first or second hand a pre-empt in diamonds could easily lead to a missed game in spades. In third position that is unlikely. Players are always reluctant to give best to a minor-suit pre-empt, so an opening Three Diamonds may act as a time bomb. The opposition will run into bad breaks whether they contest in spades or hearts.

RESPONDING TO A THREE BID

One of the costliest and commonest errors is to bid too optimistically when partner has opened with a weak bid. Players who themselves open Three bids on tram tickets are inclined to don rose-coloured spectacles when their partner has pre-empted; or perhaps it is not so much a matter of optimism as of failure to visualize the two hands in combination.

In this area of bidding there are two reliable 'don'ts'. Don't expect a partner who has pre-empted to hold any tricks at all outside his suit. And don't shop around for alternative contracts when you are strong enough to raise

partner to game or slam. As a striking example, suppose
partner opens Three Spades and you hold:

♠ –   ♡ A K 7 4 2   ◇ A J 7 3   ♣ A Q 5 4

To bid Four Hearts is idiotic, to bid Three No Trumps
criminal. You should raise to Four Spades, and if an opponent with a couple of trump tricks decides to double, see
how he savours a redouble.

Suppose, next, that partner opens Three Hearts, not
vulnerable, the next player passes, and you contemplate:

♠ Q J 9 5   ♡ 7 2   ◇ A Q 3   ♣ K J 6 2

An optimist might think, 'I've got the other suits wrapped
up,' and bid Three No Trumps. Four Hearts would be more
intelligent, but that won't be a make either. Responder
should pass smoothly, for his only chance of a killing will
occur if the opponents re-open.

As a rough guide, to make game in opener's suit you need
about 15 points opposite a non-vulnerable Three bid, 12
points when vulnerable. Moreover, these should be made up
mostly of Aces and Kings. However, it is often right to raise
as a defensive measure. Again the opening is Three Hearts,
the next player passes and you hold:

♠ 7 4   ♡ 10 5 3   ◇ A K 8 5 2   ♣ Q 4 2

You don't expect to make Four Hearts, but you hold
enough to be sure that Four Hearts doubled won't be expensive. As you cannot be sure of defeating Four Spades
it is good policy to raise, making it more hazardous for the
fourth player to compete.

LATER TACTICS

The advantage of a pre-empt is often dissipated by an im-
provident double on the part of the responder. An opening
Three Diamonds is overcalled with Three Hearts and the
next player holds:

♠ A 4 2   ♡ K J 9 7 3   ◇ 5 2   ♣ Q 10 8

It is a mistake to double. No doubt Three Hearts can be beaten – but that's not the whole apple. The opponent may have a two-suiter and either he or his partner may be glad of the hint to change course to Three Spades or possibly Three No Trumps. When partner has pre-empted the slogan is 'Don't double one contract unless you can double them all'.

Another pitfall is an ill-judged rebid by the player who has made a pre-empt. It is practically never right for a player who has pre-empted to bid again unless he has been supported by his partner. Say that you open Four Hearts on:

♠ 6   ♡ K Q 10 8 7 6 4 2   ◇ 5   ♣ Q 5 3

The next player overcalls with Four Spades and your partner doubles. In no circumstances take out into Five Hearts on the grounds that your hand will be useless in defence. You have already served notice of that.

Even when a pre-empt has been supported it is generally wrong for opener to bid again in front of his partner. Take a sequence like this:

South	West	North	East
3 ♡	3 ♠	4 ♡	4 ♠
?			

South may hold a good Three Heart bid and no defence against a spade contract, but he still must not bid Five Hearts in front of his partner. North may have raised to Four Hearts partly in the hope of pushing the enemy to Four Spades. South cannot tell from his side of the table and must pass.

Finally, if you are void of partner's suit and hold a moderate hand, pass before worse befalls. Any take-out of a Three bid is temporarily forcing and you may end up by conceding a really big penalty (known in the trade as a telephone number).

OTHER PRE-EMPTIVE BIDS

To open Four Hearts or Four Spades you need to be appreciably more than one trick stronger than when you open with a Three bid. This is because an opponent who holds two or three tricks in his own hand is much more likely to risk a speculative double when you are already in a game contract. Vulnerable, the suit must be almost immune to a bad break. Typical hands would be:

(1) ♠ 6 2   ♡ A K Q 10 8 6 3   ♢ 9 5 2   ♣ 6
(2) ♠ A Q J 9 7 5 3 2   ♡ 4   ♢ A 8   ♣ 6 2

The second hand represents the upper range for a Four bid. With anything stronger than this you risk missing a slam. In third and fourth position, of course, when partner has passed, you have much more latitude.

Pre-emptive bids may also be made after an opponent has opened the bidding. The player on your right bids One Club and you hold:

♠ K J 10 9 8 5 3   ♡ 8   ♢ Q 6 3 2   ♣ 4

Not vulnerable, an overcall of Three Spades is indicated. Note that to count as a pre-empt your bid must be a double jump. A bid of Three Diamonds over One Heart, for example, is only a single jump – not a pre-empt but a strong jump overcall as described in a later chapter.

More rarely, you may pre-empt when your own side has opened the bidding. After One Club by partner, pass by the next player, you hold:

♠ 7   ♡ K Q 10 9 7 5 2   ♢ 8 4   ♣ J 6 3

Jump to Three Hearts – one range higher than a jump shift – partly to give partner a picture of your hand, partly to make it more difficult for the opponents to contest in spades.

HOW TO COUNTER AN OPPOSING PRE-EMPT

It is convenient, while on the subject of pre-empts, to consider the best defence against them. There are many possible
methods, but modern players tend increasingly to use one
of the simplest. This is to double a Three bid for take-out
and to treat all other bids as natural. Over an opening
Three Clubs you hold:

♠ K 10 6 3   ♡ A 8 6 4 2   ◇ A Q 9   ♣ 4

This 14-point hand with support for the three unbid suits
is the irreducible minimum for a double, safe only because
partner can respond at the Three level. The next hand would
be about a minimum for a vulnerable double of Three
Spades:

♠ 7   ♡ K J 4 2   ◇ A J 7   ♣ A J 8 4 3

Suppose the bid in front of you had been Three Diamonds:
it would be unsound to double because you could not stand
a response in spades. You must pass and hope that partner
can take some action in fourth position. If the opening is
Three Hearts you may regret that you are playing 'double
for take-out', but there it is, all you can do is pass, unless
you choose to bid a very speculative Three No Trumps.

When responding to a double of a Three bid you must
call the full value of your hand, as the doubler will usually
not be able to say any more. Partner doubles an opening bid
of Three Diamonds and you hold:

(1) ♠ J 8 6 5 2   ♡ 4 2   ◇ A 8 4   ♣ K J 7
(2) ♠ J 9 6 3   ♡ A Q 4 2   ◇ 8 7 3   ♣ K 6

On the first hand you must jump to Four Spades, just as
you would jump to Two Spades in response to a double of
One Diamond. On the second hand the bid is Four Diamonds, as you have the values for game and are willing to
play in either of the major suits.

SUMMARY

Open with a pre-emptive bid when you are under strength for a bid of One but hold enough playing tricks to keep the penalty to 500.

Raise a vulnerable Three bid on 12 points, including Aces and Kings, a non-vulnerable Three bid on 15 points. Raise also on a weaker hand to maintain the pre-empt.

Double an opposition Three bid for a take-out on a hand that would represent a sound double of a bid of One.

CHAPTER 9

Coping with Intervention

The cue bid in an opponent's suit – Responding on a moderate hand – Problems in the rebid – Countering a take-out double – Doubling a suit overcall – Summary

THIS is the last of our chapters on how to bid when your side has opened. It is arguably the most important.

Most players bid competently enough when allowed a free run but are thrown off balance when opponents intervene. Thus a great many points turn on how intervention is countered. Many rubbers, and most matches, are won by the side that displays the better competitive judgement.

Although intervention is generally a hindrance it is sometimes actually helpful to the side that has opened. This occurs especially when the third player is strong enough to cue-bid the opponent's suit. This manoeuvre used to be a rarity and is still a stranger in the lives of many players. Modern players wonder how they ever got along without it.

THE CUE BID IN AN OPPONENT'S SUIT

The cue bid is a very effective move when your side holds the values for game but has not determined the best contract. Consider South's predicament in this sequence:

South	West	North	East
1♠	Pass	2♣	2♦
?			

North-South are vulnerable and South holds:

♠ A Q 10 8 3   ♡ A Q 3   ◇ J 7 4   ♣ A 5

Had there been no intervention, South would have been happy to bid Three No Trumps over Two Clubs, taking a chance on the diamonds. Now that would be foolhardy. Yet with 18 points opposite North's minimum of 9 points, there must be a game somewhere.

The solution is to cue-bid the opponent's suit, bidding Three Diamonds. This is a general-purpose force to game. It says nothing about South's holding in diamonds, except that with a reputable guard he would probably have bid No Trumps. One of the main objects of the bid is to encourage partner to indicate a guard by bidding Three No Trumps. Failing that, North will make some other descriptive bid and game will eventually be reached in one suit or another.

This type of cue bid can be used in any situation where the opponents have entered the auction. It is often used by responder on the first round. Partner opens One Club, there is a butt-in of One Spade, and you hold:

♠ 10 4 3   ♡ K 8 6 4   ◇ A 8 3   ♣ A Q 7

Now Two Spades is a life-saver.

The cue bid can still be used in the old sense, where it signified strong support for partner. You follow it up differently, that is all. Partner opens One Spade, there is a butt-in of Two Diamonds, and you hold:

♠ A Q 7 5 2   ♡ A J 6   ◇ 3   ♣ Q 10 8 2

With 16 points, this is at least a game hand in support of spades. You can express it well by overcalling Two Diamonds with Three Diamonds and bidding game in spades on the next round. The only problem would arise if partner rebid Three Spades, for then a simple raise to Four Spades would not give him a picture of the great trump support. With an average partner it would be wise to bid Five Spades.

With a sophisticated partner you could bid Four Hearts. He would interpret this as a cue bid, with spades as the agreed suit, because if you held good hearts you would force with Three Hearts over the intervening Two Diamonds. It is a mistake to cue-bid the enemy suit when you have a strong suit of your own.

Interference, then, need not cramp your style when you are strong. The problems arise when you hold a moderate responding hand. We examine that next.

RESPONDING ON A MODERATE HAND

When you hold support for partner's suit you should raise freely over intervention. If you were wondering whether to raise to Two or Three, go for the higher bid especially if good trumps are among your assets. This may present the next player with a problem. If your partner finds the contract unmakable, it is unlikely that you would have been able to buy the hand at a lower level.

These thrustful tactics are recommended only when supporting partner's suit. With a hand which is borderline for a bid in your own suit it is advisable to be more cautious. The bidding begins:

South	West	North	East
		1 ◇	1 ♡
?			

South holds: ♠ K 8 5 4   ♡ 7 6 2   ◇ 5 3   ♣ K 10 8 6

Here South would have kept the bidding open with One Spade if East had passed. There is no need for this type of 'courtesy' response when an opponent has made sure your partner will have another chance. You are not worth a 'free' bid of One Spade.

There is a good reason for the difference in tactics. When you have a fit for partner's trump suit you want to play there if possible, so you overbid a little. When no fit is assured you must bid on solid values.

It is still more important to have your feet on the ground when you would have to bid at the Two level in a suit of higher rank than the opener's suit. For example:

South	West	North	East
		1 ◇	2 ♣
?			

South holds: ♠ K J 8 6 2 ♡ K 8 2 ◇ 5 3 ♣ 7 5 2

A bid of Two Spades at this point could lead to dire trouble. Like any response in a new suit it would be forcing for one round and North would be obliged to rebid even if he held a minimum opening. The partnership could then be overboard. It is better to pass Two Clubs and see if opener can speak again. For a bid in a higher-ranking suit in this type of situation the responder needs 10 or 11 points.

When the choice is between introducing a new suit and raising opener's suit, it will usually be advisable to raise partner. You are South in the following sequence:

South	West	North	East
		1 ◇	1 ♡
?			

South holds: ♠ A J 8 3 ♡ 8 2 ◇ Q 10 7 5 ♣ 7 6 4

There may be a temptation to make a 'cheap' One-over-One bid in spades. Resist it! One Spade may turn out all right if partner can support spades, but what is more likely is that opponents will go to Two Hearts and you will have to decide whether to risk Three Diamonds, bidding a poor hand twice. The sensible course is to bid Two Diamonds on the first round, limiting your hand and giving partner the important message that you can support his suit. Having done that, you can bid Two Spades over Two Hearts without deceiving anyone.

PROBLEMS IN THE REBID

Since a free bid by responder in a new suit always shows
better than minimum values, it follows that opener should
make certain adjustments. The bidding goes:

South	West	North	East
1 ♣	1 ♡	1 ♠	Pass
?			

South holds: ♠ K 8 7 6   ♡ 4 2   ◇ A J 5   ♣ A K 8 7

Had there been no intervention this would have been a
maximum for Two Spades. As North has made a free bid
the hand is worth a raise to Three Spades.

This is another situation where the opener should bid the
full value of the combined hands:

South	West	North	East
1 ♡	2 ♣	2 ♠	Pass
?			

South holds: ♠ 6 4   ♡ A Q 5 3   ◇ A 8 4 2   ♣ K Q J

It is not sufficient for South to rebid Two No Trumps, as
he would have done after a response at the Two level in an
uninterrupted auction. Two No Trumps now would be
consistent with a minimum opening. As North has shown at
least 10 points by his response in a higher-ranking suit, and
South holds 16, South should take the pressure off his partner
by jumping to Three No Trumps.

We have been considering situations where the overcall
was made by second hand. When fourth hand intervenes,
the opener may pass a minimum hand. Clearly he will be
happy to do so in this sequence:

South	West	North	East
1 ♠	Pass	2 ◇	2 ♡
?			

South holds: ♠ K 8 5 3 2   ♡ A 4   ◇ 8 6   ♣ A J 8 3

When South opened One Spade he did not exactly relish the idea of having to rebid Two Spades over a response at the Two level. Now that East has intervened, South can pass. Any free rebid would suggest additional values.

With a strong hand the opener's best weapon on the second round, assuming his partner has not made a bid, is a take-out double. Here are two typical situations where a double is for take-out:

(1)	*South*	*West*	*North*	*East*
	1 ♡	2 ♣	Pass	Pass
	Double			
(2)	*South*	*West*	*North*	*East*
	1 ♡	Pass	Pass	2 ◇
	Double			

Clearly South needs to be stronger for the second double than for the first. In the protective position he might reopen with a double on 15 points. In the second sequence he needs at least 17, for with a partner who has passed a One bid he is very much under the hammer.

When the values are present for a take-out double, this tends to be the best move. Suppose that after the first sequence above South holds:

♠ K J 5   ♡ A K 5 3 2   ◇ A J 9 6   ♣ 4

South has opened One Heart and there has been an over-call on his left of Two Clubs, followed by two passes. A double is much more flexible than a rebid of Two Hearts or Two Diamonds. Among the options it keeps open is that of a penalty pass by partner.

COUNTERING A TAKE-OUT DOUBLE

Especially important is the action by third hand after a take-out double by second hand. The standard way to show strength is to redouble. For this you need at least 9 or 10 high-card points. The redouble does not promise strength in partner's suit; on the contrary, the manoeuvre is the more effective when you are short in opener's suit and are plotting to penalize the opposition.

This is a good hand for a redouble after partner's One Spade has been doubled for a take-out:

♠ 9   ♡ K J 9 4 2   ◇ 7 5 2   ♣ A Q 8 3

Don't be worried by the singleton spade. It is most unlikely that your partner will be left to play in One Spade redoubled, and even then he may make it. On the basis of your redouble your partner may be able to double Two Diamonds and you can double anything else.

Study the next sequence carefully, for the free rebid by the opener has a different meaning from the free rebid when there has been a suit overcall.

South	West	North	East
1 ♠	Double	Redouble	2 ♣
2 ♠			

South's bid of Two Spades says: 'I'm not giving you a chance to double Two Clubs as I could not stand such a double. I hold a weakish hand with a long spade suit.' The message would be the same if East had passed over the redouble.

Other tactical moves over a double of your partner's opening bid are as follows:

Direct raises of opener's suit are pre-emptive. One Spade–Double–Three Spades is an attempted shut-out. (With a genuine raise to Three, redouble first.)

A simple bid in a new suit is not forcing. Such a bid is qualified by the failure to redouble.

A jump shift is forcing for one round only. One Club–Double–Two Spades suggests a good suit and about 11 to 13 points. A redouble would serve no useful purpose as you do not propose to play for penalties.

One No Trump shows 7 to 9 points. You may also pass with

this degree of strength. The main object of the bid is often to prevent the fourth player from responding at the One level.

DOUBLING A SUIT OVERCALL

It may surprise you that in good company the juiciest penalties arise from doubles of low contracts rather than high ones. After several rounds of bidding, players have a good idea of how many tricks they are likely to make and whether a sacrifice will be worth taking. On the other hand, a player may make a reasonable overcall on the first round and run into stacked trumps or a useless dummy.

At a low level your holding in partner's suit is almost as important as your holding in the suit you propose to double. It is hardly ever right to double with four or more cards in partner's suit and seldom right with three. Ideal is a doubleton or singleton. A void is less good, partly because you will have to look elsewhere for an opening lead and partly because partner may not be able to develop the suit by himself.

One further small surprise: the best trump holding for a double is four cards in the opponent's suit, not a long string of six or seven. Indeed, many good penalties follow a double on three cards.

A double with five or more trumps will seldom lead to anything as such a double seldom sticks. Someone, most likely your partner, will hold a void and remove the double. For tactical reasons it is a mistake to double on trump tricks alone: the opponents may try another contract and your partner may double this without success. It is also seldom good tactics to double at the range of One. Wait for better things.

The next important question is when to stand partner's double and when to remove it. You should normally accept a double of an overcall when you have a doubleton in trumps. You should certainly take out when you are void. Beware the fallacious argument, 'As I am void of trumps my partner must be stuffed with them'. More often, partner's trumps are sandwiched between declarer and dummy. Also, being void, you can never lead a trump and this may snarl up the defence.

The borderline decisions arise when you hold a singleton in the suit that has been doubled. So long as you have your normal ration of defensive tricks you should pass unless you are two-suited. The bidding begins:

South	West	North	East
1 ♠	2 ♣	Double	Pass
?			

South holds:

(1) ♠ K J 8 7 4 ♡ A Q 9 4 2 ◇ 6 3 ♣ Q

(2) ♠ K Q J 4 3 ♡ A 8 4 ◇ Q 6 4 2 ♣ 6

On the first hand South should remove to Two Hearts. There are two good reasons: (*a*) his hand may not be much help against the contract of Two Clubs; (*b*) his partner, who is no doubt short in spades, may have good support for hearts.

The second hand is a minimum opening, but that by itself is no reason for taking out the double. If partner has a singleton spade your hand may be useful in defence. It would be foolish to take out into Two Spades and you have no other suit worth calling.

SUMMARY

Cue-bid the opponent's suit when your side holds the values for game but has not determined the best spot to play in.

Raise freely in competition but do not introduce new suits on borderline hands.

When partner's opening bid is doubled for take-out, redouble to show at least 9 or 10 high-card points.

The ideal holding for a double of an overcall is four trumps and a singleton or doubleton in partners' suit. Stand your partner's double unless you are void of trumps or have a two-suiter or hold less than the normal ration of defensive tricks.

Part Two

The Contested Auction

CHAPTER 10

The Take-out Double

When to double – Responding to a double – Re-bidding after you have doubled – Doubling after you have passed – Doubling in fourth position – Summary

THE most settled, immutable, transfixed and stubborn convention in bridge is the take-out double. It means the same now as it did when contract bridge was invented. It has the same meaning in every country and in every system.

The reason for its durability is simple. The take-out double, as a means of reaching the best contract after opponents have opened, has demonstrable advantages over any other form of action. An additional merit is that it does not displace any useful call. It could hardly ever be intelligent to double an opening bid for penalties: such a double would either be unrewarding or would cause the opponents to hie themselves to a better spot.

So a double at a low level does not mean 'I think we can beat this call'. The message is 'I hold at least the equivalent of an opening bid. It is quite possible that the hand belongs to us. Tell me where your values lie.'

The take-out double is especially useful when you have no fixed ideas where you want to end up. Say that the bidding has been opened on your right with a bid of One Spade and you hold:

♠ 10   ♡ K J 5 3 2   ◇ K Q 7   ♣ A J 8 2

There are two objections to an overcall of Two Hearts. First, it is not safe, you might run into a penalty double.

Secondly, you are not giving your side much chance to find a contract in one of the minors, which might be much better than a contract in hearts. A sound partner will not introduce a suit such as Q J x x x x in a competitive situation unless you invite him to do so with a take-out double.

By doubling One Spade you keep every possibility open. You may play in any one of three suits or in No Trumps. You may even defend against One Spade doubled, on the rare occasion when partner holds a string of spades and elects to pass the double.

Because of its flexibility and effectiveness modern players use the take-out double in very many situations. We illustrate these in the remainder of this chapter.

WHEN TO DOUBLE

The first point to determine is when a double is for take-out and not for penalties. You won't go wrong if you commit this rule to memory:

A double of a suit contract at part-score level is for take-out provided that (1) partner has not made a positive bid and (2) the double is made at the first opportunity.

Note that this definition does not include doubles of One No Trump. A double of One No Trump is primarily for penalties and the partner should take it out only if he is weak and unbalanced.

Here is the simplest example of a take-out double:

South	West	North	East
Pass	Pass	1 ♠	Double

West's pass does not qualify as a 'positive bid', so the double, which is made at the first opportunity, is for take-out. But how about this next sequence?

South	West	North	East
Pass	1 ♢	1 ♠	Double

This double is for penalties, because West has already given some indication of where his values lie. The next situation is more tricky.

South	West	North	East
Pass	Pass	1 ♡	Pass
2 ♣	Double		

West is asking for a take-out even though he has previously passed. This is his first opportunity of doubling. Finally:

South	West	North	East
1 ♡	Pass	1 NT	Pass
2 ♡	Double		

West's double is for penalties as he could have doubled for a take-out on the first round.

Slightly different rules apply to a double in the protective position – that is to say, a double when the last bid has been followed by two passes.

South	West	North	East
Pass	Pass	1 ♡	Pass
2 ◇	Pass	Pass	Double

This would be a take-out double, the presumption being that East passed on the first round because he had values in hearts and was not prepared for a take-out into diamonds. Now that the opponents have bid diamonds and have subsided at a low level, East decides to fight for the part score.

The ideal hand for an immediate double is one containing support for all the unbid suits. The distributions 4-4-4-1 and 5-4-4-0 obviously fulfil this requirement, and 5-4-3-1 is just as good in practice. With such distribution (the opponent having bid your short suit, of course) you need only 11 or 12 high-card points. When the pattern is not so good the minimum is from 13 to 15, depending on various factors.

Such considerations as vulnerability, the rank of the suits, and whether or not partner has passed, are all important. Suppose the opening bid on your right is One Spade and you hold:

♠ 8 3   ♡ K J 4   ◇ A J 6 4   ♣ K Q 7 3

Vulnerable, you would be wise to pass. You are asking partner to bid a suit at the Two level and in particular to bid the other major, for which you have poor support. If the opening bid were One Club and your doubleton was in clubs, the double would be perfectly sound.

Mention of the 'other major' touches on a very important point. In response to a double, partner will always give priority to a major suit, sometimes bidding a four-card major in front of a five-card minor. It follows that with good major suits you can lower the requirements to rock-bottom.

♠ K J 7 3   ♡ Q 10 6 4 2   ◇ A 9 6   ♣ 4

It is fair to double One Club. This is the sort of hand we had in mind when we said that the minimum for a double was 11 points.

Here is one more example to show how important is the rank of the suits.

♠ K J 8   ♡ A 10 6   ◇ 8 2   ♣ A J 5 4 3

Over One Spade you should pass, for you have poor support for diamonds and moderate support for the other major. The club suit is unattractive for an overcall at the Two level. But if the opening bid were One Diamond you could double. Partner will not assume that you necessarily hold four cards in whatever major suit he wants to bid.

Some players will tell you never to double if your hand contains a singleton or doubleton in one of the unbid suits. That may be sound advice for a beginner but not for an experienced player who is capable of taking into account the rank of the suits. An opponent opens One Spade and you hold:

♠ A 4 3   ♡ A J 5 4   ◇ A J 7 6 4   ♣ 8

A double is reasonably safe because over a response of Two Clubs you can bid Two Diamonds.

With the next hand you would have an awkward decision over One Diamond:

♠ A J 8 3 2   ♡ K J 7 4   ◇ A 10 2   ♣ 6

You would like to double, holding good support for both majors, but would not be well placed over a response of Two Clubs. It would exaggerate your strength to continue with Two Spades. On the whole it is better to overcall with One Spade on the first round.

Doubling on a strong hand of 17 points or more. With this strength you should double on most hands that are not suitable for an overcall of One No Trump or a jump in a suit (see Chapter Eleven). It is still a mistake to double one major suit with a singleton of the other, for your partner may be 'bounced' into a contract for which you are wholly unprepared. The correct action on such hands will usually be to pass. The opponent on your right opens One Spade and you hold:

♠ K J 8 4   ♡ 3   ◇ A K 8 4   ♣ K Q 6 3

If you double you may find yourself in Four Hearts when the bidding next comes round. Best is a 'trap pass', giving the opponents rope with which to hang themselves.

Doubling when both opponents have bid. We have been concerned so far with immediate doubles by second hand. You may also make a take-out double after either of these sequences:

	South	West	North	East
(1)	1♠	Pass	3♠	Double
(2)	South	West	North	East
	1♡	Pass	2♣	Double

In the second sequence there is a strong inference that East has good support for both unbid suits. Without such support he should pass, as the sequence is forcing for the opposition and East will have another chance to decide whether or not to enter the auction.

RESPONDING TO A DOUBLE

When responding to a double you should think of your hand as being either weak (0–8) points, medium (9–11), or strong.

Responding on weak hands, 0 to 8 points. Almost the greatest gaffe a player can commit is to pass from weakness. Suppose that at game all One Spade is doubled and you hold in response:

♠ 8 6 4 2   ♡ 9 5 3   ◇ 1 0 7 4   ♣ 8 3 2

You must grit your teeth and bid Two Clubs. Whatever this costs in the end, it will be less than letting them make One Spade doubled with overtricks at 200 a time.

Having cleared the air on that point, we can turn to more positive advice. In general, you should bid your best suit at the lowest level. Bid a four-card major at the level of One in preference to a five-card minor at the level of Two.

The most awkward hands are those where your only four-card suit is the one that has been doubled. Partner doubles One Heart and you hold:

♠ J 8 3   ♡ J 8 5 4   ◇ 7 6 2   ♣ Q 9 5

One Spade is a better response than One No Trump, which suggests a slightly better hand in the 6 to 8 range.

If the opponent on your right calls over the double you are absolved from responding. However, partner has asked you for news and if there is anything you can tell him you should do so. The bidding goes:

South	West	North	East
1 ◇	Double	Redouble	?

East holds: ♠ 8   ♡ J 9 6 3   ◇ Q 5 4 3 2   ♣ 10 7 6

East should bid One Heart and not wait for his partner to bid One Spade and perhaps be doubled in that. West should not assume that One Heart shows any positive strength.

Responding on medium hands, 9 to 11 points. A hand of this strength will often produce game opposite a take-out double. Responder should signify this by a jump, encouraging but not forcing. As always, the likelihood of a good or bad fit must be taken into account. Two examples will show the kind of thinking that is needed.

(1)	South	West	North	East
	Pass	1 ♡	Double	Pass
	?			

South holds: ♠ Q J 9 4   ♡ 7 6 2   ◇ J 7   ♣ K Q 10 4

Only 9 points, but there are good features – four cards in the unbid major and no points in hearts, where presumably partner is short. Also, South has previously passed. He should jump to Two Spades now.

(2)	South	West	North	East
		1 ♡	Double	Pass
	?			

South holds: ♠ J 6 3   ♡ Q 5   ◇ A 9 6 2   ♣ K 8 4 3

Here South holds 10 points, but the Queen of hearts may be wasted and there is no good suit. Two Clubs would be an underbid and the best response may be One No Trump, despite the lack of a guard in hearts. As East has not supported the hearts it is likely that North holds an honour, and in that case South's Queen will be most useful.

Responding on strong hands, 12 points or more. If your hand is close to an opening bid it must be worth a game call opposite a take-out double. With a long suit you may bid the game direct. Partner doubles One Diamond and you hold:

♠ A 4   ♡ Q J 9 6 4 3   ◇ 8 5   ♣ K 6 2

With 10 points in high cards and 2 for distribution, the bid is Four Hearts.

With a guard in the opponent's suit and a long minor you should think in terms of No Trumps. In response to a double of One Spade you hold:

♠ K 10 6   ♡ 5 3   ◇ K Q 8 6 4 2   ♣ Q 6

Jump to Three No Trumps. No doubt partner controls the hearts and your diamonds should run for six tricks.

When your destination is uncertain the solution is to cue-bid the enemy suit. Partner doubles One Diamond and you hold:

♠ K J 8 3   ♡ A 8 4   ◇ 5 2   ♣ K Q 7 4

Clearly any direct game bid may put you in the wrong contract. Return the ball to partner's court with a bid of Two Diamonds. Then both players can advance gradually until a fit is found.

The penalty pass. We stressed above that you must never pass a take-out double from panic. The only time you should pass is when you hold such good trumps that you can expect to defeat the opponents in a contract at the One level. For this, a really solid sequence is needed, such as Q J 10 9 6 4. A straggly assortment like K J x x x x will die several deaths when under declarer's A Q 10 8 5.

After a penalty pass the game for the defence is to pick up declarer's low trumps by force. The doubler should therefore lead a trump if he has one.

South	West	North	East
1 ♡	Double	Pass	Pass
Pass			

West holds: ♠ A K 10 4   ♡ 5   ◇ Q J 10 8   ♣ A 7 4 2

West should reject the attractive alternatives and lead his singleton heart.

REBIDDING AFTER YOU HAVE DOUBLED

When you have doubled you are not obliged to rebid unless partner cue-bids the enemy suit. It is easy to fall into the trap of bidding the same values twice over. You double One Spade, partner responds Two Hearts, and you hold:

♠ 6   ♡ A Q 7 4   ◇ K J 8 4   ♣ A 9 6 2

This may seem pleasant but you must take into account that partner may have been forced to respond on a weak hand with only four hearts. A spade lead and continuation, forcing your hand to ruff, could be very awkward. You should pass Two Hearts.

This time you double One Diamond and partner responds One Spade. You hold:

♠ K J 8 6   ♡ A 9 4   ◇ 6   ♣ A Q 7 3 2

Don't think that summer has come and leap to Four Spades. Again, partner could be very weak and a diamond lead and continuation would force him to lead away from your hand. A raise to Two Spades is enough.

If you double and follow with a bid of a new suit, partner will know you are strong, so it is seldom necessary to jump. To double and follow with a bid of No Trumps suggests about 18 points, a hand too strong for a One No Trump overcall.

DOUBLING AFTER YOU HAVE PASSED

A player who has passed originally has much scope for doubling on a well-distributed hand.

South	West	North	East
Pass	1 ◇	Pass	1 ♡
Double			

South holds: ♠ K 10 7 4   ♡ A 4 2   ◇ 6   ♣ Q J 7 3 2

South has just what his partner will expect – a hand not far short of an opening bid with good support for both unbid suits.

Even when you have passed it is unsound to double on distribution alone. When you have shape but no tricks you may have recourse to the 'unusual' No Trump, described in Chapter Twelve.

DOUBLING IN FOURTH POSITION

When an opening bid is followed by two passes the fourth player, holding a fair hand, is in a favourable position to double.

South	West	North	East
	1 ♡	Pass	Pass
?			

South holds: ♠ Q 9 7 6   ♡ 4   ◇ A 10 5   ♣ A K 8 4 2

South should double as he is well prepared for any action his partner may take. A penalty pass is now a live possibility, for K J 9 x x in the trump suit *over* the declarer has much appeal.

The fourth player may also double on weaker hands than this. The general standard for any form of action is less than for the same action by the second player. It is right to double on most hands of 11 points upwards.

SUMMARY

A double is for take-out when partner has not made a positive bid and the contract is below game level.

The minimum standard for a double by second hand ranges from 11 to 15 points, depending on vulnerabilty, distribution, and the rank of the suit involved.

When responding to a double, bid your longest suit at minimum level on 0–8 points, jump from 9–11, and with upwards of 12 bid game or cue-bid the opponent's suit. Pass for penalties only with a very strong trump holding.

CHAPTER 11

The Overcall

*The space theory – The simple overcall – Responding
to an overcall – Protective bidding – One No Trump
overcall – Jump overcall – Summary*

SEVERAL times in the course of a session you will find yourself wondering whether or not to overcall an opponent's
opening bid. Bundles of points will hang on it – yet few
players give more than a passing thought to the problems
involved.

If you were asked your motive for overcalling you would
have to think. You might come up with any or all of these
answers:

(1) To suggest a good line of defence should the opponents
play the hand.

(2) To buy the contract should it turn out that your side
can outbid the opposition.

(3) To discover a fit with partner that may enable you to
sacrifice cheaply or even push the opponents overboard.

These are all worthy objectives, though for our part we
rank the first one – suggesting a lead – rather low. It becomes
relevant only if your partner is on lead – and then only if
he is incapable of finding a good opening on his own.

The second motive for overcalling – that you hope to
buy the contract and make it – can be prominent only if
you hold a fairly strong hand. On most such hands you will
enter with a take-out double rather than a simple overcall.

The third possibility – that even if outgunned you may be
able to 'push' successfully – is the most important of the
three. A flair for pushing is one of the greatest assets a cut-in

player can have. We devote a special section to this in a
later chapter.

THE SPACE THEORY

We have given three reasons for overcalling, but there is a
fourth, considered by modern players to be as important
as any. This is to deprive the opponents of bidding space.
The simple fact is that your opponents will usually find it
easier to reach their best contract if allowed a free run than
if they have to cope with intervention.

Any overcall is liable to inconvenience the opposition, but
the most effective is one that consumes bidding space. If
opponents are allowed to develop gradually by way of One
Club–One Diamond–One Heart–One No Trump, etc,
they will bid accurately; but if over One Club you can
interject One Spade they may have problems. You deny
them the chance to develop at leisure, and just that little
nudge may push them off the rails.

Players with a good competitive sense take the space
factor very much into account. Over an opening bid of
One Club on your right you might make a non-vulnerable
overcall of One Spade on a hand as weak as:

$$\spadesuit A J 8 6 \quad \heartsuit 7 3 \quad \diamondsuit K 10 4 2 \quad \clubsuit 8 6 5$$

Note that if the opening bid were One Heart an overcall
of One Spade would occupy no bidding space and would be
unjustified on so weak a hand.

A bid of Two Clubs over an opponent's One Diamond
opening can also be very effective. The overcall cuts out
both major suits and also One No Trump. It is justified, not
vulnerable, on as moderate a hand as:

$$\spadesuit 9 7 4 \quad \heartsuit 8 2 \quad \diamondsuit K 3 \quad \clubsuit K J 9 7 6 3$$

This kind of overcall will run into an occasional 700, we
admit. Never mind! It will lead to many invisible gains when
the opponents are kept out of their best game contract.

Such, then, are the objectives. The next step is to devise a scheme that will give effect to them.

THE SIMPLE OVERCALL

The simple non-jump overcall in a suit is by far the most common type of intervention. We begin with a few negative injunctions.

Do not make a simple overcall on hands containing 15 points or more. On these hands prefer One No Trump or a jump overcall or a double.

Do not make a simple overcall when much of your strength is in the opponent's suit. For example, One Heart is opened on your right and you hold:

♠ Q 8   ♡ K J 9 3   ◊ A 10 8 6 2   ♣ 6 3

You are strong in defence and if you concede a penalty you will be saving nothing. We met a similar situation when discussing take-out doubles. You should pass and hope the opponents run into trouble.

We are left with hands of, say, 8 to 14 points, either one-suited or two-suited. Here the correct action will depend mainly on how good a suit you hold.

1. *You hold a fairly good five-card or longer suit.*

With this type of suit, A J 10 x x or better, you may overcall either at the One or Two level. For a vulnerable overcall at the Two level you need to be in the upper bracket both in points and playing tricks. Suppose that One Heart is opened on your right and you hold:

♠ 8 5 4   ♡ K 7   ◊ A 10 3   ♣ K Q J 8 3

This would be an irreducible minimum for a vulnerable overcall at the Two level. With one more club you could dispense with the King of hearts; a six-card suit makes a big difference.

2. *You hold a biddable four-card suit or a weak five-card suit.*

With this type of suit you may overcall at the One level but not at the Two level. If vulnerable, the four-card suit should be strong, not less than K Q 10 x.

On minimum hands, 8 to 10 points and only a moderate suit, ask yourself these questions:

(*a*) Does the overcall rob the opponents of bidding space?

(*b*) Is the vulnerability favourable, so that the overcall may lead to a cheap sacrifice?

If you cannot answer 'Yes' to either question it will be better to pass.

RESPONDING TO AN OVERCALL

The responses to an overcall are more blunt than to an opening bid. There is neither time nor space for delicate approach. A simple change of suit is not forcing, so cannot be used as an exploratory move. Even a jump in a new suit is forcing for only one round. The only game-forcing response is a cue bid in the opponent's suit.

As it is difficult to explore accurately in a competitive auction, there is a greater tendency to raise partner's suit. This may be done freely on three-card support and even on a doubleton when the overcall is at the Two level.

There is a marked difference in the standard of No Trump responses, as compared with the responses to an opening bid. You may respond One No Trump to partner's non-vulnerable overcall on as much as 12 points, and you should bid only Two No Trumps on 13 or 14. A vulnerable overcall may be treated as almost equal to an opening bid, enabling you to respond One No Trump on 8 to 10, Two No Trumps on 11 to 13. These figures are only a rough guide, for much depends on the fit with partner's suit and the nature of the guard in the opponent's suit. A guard such as J 10 x x tends to be more effective than A x x.

And what if your partner's overcall is doubled? You

should not rescue merely because you are short in his suit.
Here is an example of the worst type of rescue:

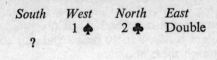

South	West	North	East
	1 ♠	2 ♣	Double
?			

South holds: ♠ 8 7 6 3   ♡ A 6 3   ◇ A 10 7 3 2   ♣ 2

South should not dream of removing the double. His two
Aces will surely be of assistance in Two Clubs. Furthermore,
North's clubs are doubtless better than South's diamonds.
(It is true that North's diamonds may be better than South's
clubs, but that is only speculation.)

A rescue would be permissible, after the same bidding, on
this type of hand:

♠ J 7 3   ♡ Q J 8 4 3 2   ◇ 10 8   ♣ 5 2

Here you have two cards of partner's suit, but because of
their low rank they won't be of much assistance. You can be
pretty sure that your hand will be useless in Two Clubs
doubled. On the other hand, partner is likely to hold some
high cards that will be of use to you in a heart contract.
Clinching the issue is a quite subtle point: opponents will
be much less trigger-happy when there is a risk of doubling
you into game.

Another type of rescue, the S O S redouble, is described
in the next chapter.

PROTECTIVE BIDDING

When an opening bid is followed by two passes the average
standard for any call by fourth hand is lower than for the
same call by second hand. This is particularly true of the
simple overcall, which in the protective position seldom
shows more than about 9 to 12 points. The bidding goes:

South	West	North	East
	1 ◊	Pass	Pass
?			

The question is whether South should reopen on a hand of this sort:

♠ J 5 2   ♡ A Q 4 2   ◊ 6 4   ♣ Q 10 8 2

Players who make reckless overcalls in second position tend to suffer nameless fears when in fourth position. With the present hand they would say to themselves:

'There can hardly be a game for us, and if I reopen with One Heart I give them a chance to get together in spades. A contract of One Diamond won't take them far, so I am going to pass.'

A shrewder assessment would be:

'East must be very weak to pass his partner's opening bid. My partner may have passed a fair hand, especially if he holds strength in diamonds. There is a good chance that we hold the balance of the cards. I'll accept the slight risk that they may be able to outbid us in spades and will contest with One Heart.'

South in this example is said to be in the protective position because one of the reasons for bidding is to protect a possible strong pass by his partner. It is good style to reopen with a take-out double on any fairish hand, as partner may be able to pass for penalty.

One No Trump in fourth position is a limited bid with a range of 11 to 14 at any vulnerability. The bidding goes:

South	West	North	East
	1 ♠	Pass	Pass
?			

South holds: ♠ Q 5   ♡ A Q 4   ◊ K J 8 5   ♣ 10 6 3 2

The best call is One No Trump. There is nearly always advantage in forcing the stronger opponent to make the opening lead. In this instance partner may hold A x x or K x x in spades, creating a sure double stop.

A different type of protection occurs when both opponents have bid but have let the bidding die at a low level. Paradoxically, a bid at the Two level may be justified now on a hand that would have been unsafe to call at the One level. With both sides vulnerable the bidding goes:

South	West	North	East
			1 ◇
Pass	2 ◇	Pass	Pass
?			

South holds: ♠ K 3   ♡ Q 8 5 3 2   ◇ 7 5   ♣ A 7 6 4

An overcall of One Heart on the first round would have been unsound on this assortment, but it is perfectly reasonable now to contest with Two Hearts. It is unlikely that this will be doubled, and partner will not be misled as your hand is limited by the failure to bid on the first round.

As a general rule, be reluctant to let your opponents subside at the level of One or Two. Try to push them to the Three level, where you may stand a sporting chance of defeating them.

There remain two types of overcall which can be discussed quite briefly because they conform to a clear pattern.

ONE NO TRUMP OVERCALL

To overcall an opening bid with One No Trump you require about 15 to 17 points, including a guard in the opponent's suit. (With a weaker balanced hand you should pass.) When vulnerable, do not overcall on a minimum unless you have an escape suit. The One No Trump overcall is in fact often accompanied by a five-card minor.

♠ Q 5   ♡ K J 8   ◇ A 6 2   ♣ K Q 6 4 2

Over an opening One Heart, One No Trump is more purposeful and descriptive than Two Clubs.

With upwards of 18 points the scheme is to double first and bid No Trumps over the response. For an immediate overcall of Two No Trumps see the 'unusual' No Trump in the next chapter.

JUMP OVERCALL

A jump overcall, Two Spades over One Diamond, or Three Clubs over One Heart, indicates a six-card suit in a hand which is above the 14-point maximum for a simple overcall. The usual range is about 15 to 17, including distribution. This hand would be typical:

♠ A Q 10 8 7 4   ♥ 5   ♦ A Q 8   ♣ J 9 2

Overcall any One bid with Two Spades. This is not forcing. With a still stronger hand – say with ♣ K Q x instead of J x x – double first and bid the long suit on the next round.

SUMMARY

With 8 to 14 points make a simple overcall if you hold a reasonable quota of tricks. With minimum hands consider whether you will be robbing the opponents of bidding space.

With 15 to 17 points, either (a) make a jump overcall on a six-card suit, or (b) bid One No Trump on a balanced hand, or (c) double for take-out, or (d) make a trap pass when you are strong in the opponent's suit and have no good overcall.

With upwards of 18 points usually double for take-out. (See also 'cue bids' in the next chapter.)

In fourth position bid One No Trump on 11 to 14 and lower the requirements for all other forms of action.

CHAPTER 12

Conventional Moves in Defence

The S O S redouble – The cue bid – The 'unusual' No Trump – Lead-directing doubles – Lightner slam double – Summary

MOST bidding gadgets are designed for the uncontested auction. In the hurly-burly of a competitive sequence there is seldom time for conventional manoeuvres. Nevertheless, a small number of conventions have gained acceptance because they employ 'idle' bids that are scarcely ever needed in a natural sense. The ones we describe are used the world over by good players but it would be unwise to deploy any of them in a cut-in game with a strange partner.

THE SOS REDOUBLE

The S O S redouble is not exactly a call for all seasons – most four-figure penalties result from its misinterpretation – but with a reliable partner it will enable you to dig your way out of many a boothole. It can be used both by the player who has been doubled and by his partner.

A redouble is for rescue when made at a low level and when it is clear from the general situation that the player cannot be strong enough for the 'we-can-make-it' type of redouble.

South	West	North	East
1 ♠	1 NT	Double	Pass
Pass	Redouble		

Clearly West, having made a normal overcall on 15 to 17 points, cannot be saying, 'I know we can make it.' He probably has only a single guard in spades and judges it advisable to seek a fit in one of his four-card suits.

In the next sequence the S O S redouble is employed by the side that has opened the bidding.

South	West	North	East
1 NT	Pass	Pass	Double
Pass	Pass	Redouble	

There are not enough points in the pack for South to open One No Trump, East to double, West to make a penalty pass, and North to say, 'We've got them on the run.' North has a weak hand and wants South to bid a suit.

A player who is 4-4-4-1 will sometimes bid his short suit with the intention of redoubling for a rescue. This may be the best way to find a fit in one of the other suits. Thus in the example above, North might bid Two Clubs on a singleton and redouble for a rescue.

The redouble can also be extended to situations where the redoubler could in theory hold a strong hand, but where he would be content to pass if he fancied the doubled contract. The commonest example is when partner has been doubled in a simple overcall, as in this sequence:

South	West	North	East
1 ♡	2 ♢	Double	Redouble

If East is strong he will be content to make overtricks in the doubled contract, so it is more useful to play this redouble as a cry for rescue. The possibility of playing in the opponent's heart suit is not excluded. If East passed over the double of Two Diamonds and West redoubled, the meaning would be the same.

THE CUE BID

The strongest overcall is a bid of the opponent's suit, Two

Hearts over One Heart. It may be used on any hand which is powerful enough to offer a reasonable play for game opposite a very weak dummy. It is particularly useful on big two-suiters and on other hands where there is an objection to a take-out double. Suppose One Diamond is opened on your right and you hold:

    (1) ♠ A Q J 7 4 ♡ K 5 ◇ – ♣ A K 10 6 4 2
    (2) ♠ A K 4 ♡ K Q J 8 6 ◇ 5 ♣ A K Q 9
    (3) ♠ 4 ♡ A K Q J 8 6 ◇ A 4 ♣ A 9 3 2

In each case the best move is to overcall with a cue bid of Two Diamonds. Partner will respond in his best suit, just as he would to take-out double.

The cue bid in opponent's suit is by tradition forcing to game. The modern technique is to allow a player to pass when his suit has been supported to a limited degree. Observe these two sequences:

(1)	South	West	North	East
	1 ◇	2 ◇	Pass	2 ♡
	Pass	3 ♡	Pass	?

East may pass on a very weak hand.

(2)	South	West	North	East
	1 ◇	2 ◇	Pass	2 ♡
	Pass	2 ♠	Pass	2 NT
	Pass	3 ♣	Pass	3 ♠
	Pass	?		

East was obliged to keep the bidding open over Two Spades and over Three Clubs, but now West is permitted to pass Three Spades.

It must also be remarked that among good players a cue bid following a take-out double has changed its meaning over the years.

South	West	North	East
1 ♡	Double	No	2 ◇
No	2 ♡		

This used to be the standard way of showing length in the enemy suit and intention to play there. Now it is simply a request for further information. West may hold:

♠ A K 6 2   ♡ K 4   ◇ A Q 3   ♣ K Q J 4

As in most cases where a defender bids the enemy suit, West is interested in any further move his partner can make.

THE 'UNUSUAL' NO TRUMP

New ideas in bidding do not always commend themselves to experienced players, most of whom are as lazy as the next man, but this modern convention made an immediate impact on both sage and stripling. It contains such explosive elements that you certainly ought to know about it, if only for self-protection.

As with all good conventions, the 'unusual' No Trump finds employment for a bid that would have no useful application in its normal sense. Take a sequence like this:

South	West	North	East
Pass	Pass	Pass	1 ♠
1 NT			

As South has already passed, he cannot hold the necessary strength for a genuine overcall of One No Trump. Someone had the bright idea of saying: 'Let's use the bid of No Trumps in such a situation to show a pronounced minor two-suiter. If partner can support either suit there may be a good sacrifice.'

This was a sound notion and it quickly caught on. Aficionados now recognize many situations where a bid of No Trumps is unusual and so contains a special meaning, not always tied to the minor suits. These are some examples:

(1)	South	West	North	East
	1 ◇	2 NT		

West might in theory hold the values for a genuine Two No Trumps, but it is unlikely and anyway such a hand can equally well be introduced with a double. Thus an overcall of Two No Trumps, even when not preceded by a pass, is classified as 'unusual' by all who follow the convention. In this case it would denote a two-suiter in the lowest unbid suits, hearts and clubs.

(2)	South	West	North	East
	1 ♡	2 ♣	2 ♡	Pass
	Pass	2 NT		

A genuine Two No Trumps is not consistent with the previous simple overcall of Two Clubs. West is saying, 'I hold good diamonds in addition to my club suit. Perhaps we can defend in one of these suits?' He would hold something like:

♠ K 4   ♡ 6   ◇ A 10 7 5   ♣ K Q 10 8 6 2

This would not be suitable for an immediate overcall of Two No Trumps because the diamonds are not long enough.

We turn now to some lead-directing stratagems. First, a situation where the penalty double of a game contract conveys a special message.

LEAD-DIRECTING DOUBLES

Against a No Trump contract, particularly, the opening lead can make a difference of several tricks. Sometimes it is worth taking quite a big risk in order to get the right lead. Consider this sequence:

South	West	North	East
		1 ♣	Pass
2 NT	Pass	3 NT	Double
Pass	Pass	Pass	

As West, what inference would you draw? Your partner has passed over One Club, yet has doubled Three No

Trumps. It is not difficult to work out what is going on. Obviously East has very strong clubs and wants you to lead a club against Three No Trumps. He may hold ♣ K Q J 10 x and a quick entry.

That is a clear example of a lead-directing double. In the course of time certain conventional understandings have developed.

When either the doubler or his partner has bid a suit, the double asks for that suit to be led. When both have bid, the doubler asks for his own suit.

When the doubling side has not entered the auction, as in the example above, the double usually asks for the first suit by dummy.

These are only general guides and common-sense takes priority over any rule. Consider this sequence:

South	West	North	East
Pass	1 ◇	Pass	1 ♠
Pass	2 ◇	Pass	2 NT
Pass	3 NT	Double	Pass
Pass	Pass		

The significant fact here is that West has bid diamonds twice, and as both players made limited bids on the second round it is fair to suppose that East will need to make tricks out of the diamond suit in No Trumps. This is not a lead-directing double, therefore; no doubt North has some tricks in diamonds but it cannot be sensible to attack dummy's suit. South should make his normal lead.

It is possible on occasion to make a lead-directing double when no suit has been mentioned. The bidding goes:

South	West	North	East
1 NT	Pass	3 NT	Double
Pass	Pass	Pass	

What is afoot? It is very unlikely that East, not on lead, has enough strength in his own hand to be sure of defeating a freely bid game in No Trumps. He is trying to convey this message: 'If you can find the right lead we can beat this contract, because I have a set-up suit. Don't lead any suit in which you hold length or a high honour. Try to find my suit.' East may hold:

♠ 7   ♥ J 9 4   ♦ A K Q J 8   ♣ 10 6 4 2

If West can pick on a diamond lead the story ends happily.

LIGHTNER SLAM DOUBLE

The Lightner slam double has been around for thirty years and no one has so far found a word to say against it!

The idea is that the double of a freely bid slam contract should convey the message: 'Please find an *unexpected* lead: not any suit that we have bid, not the unbid suit, not a trump.' The double is used by a player who holds a void somewhere or perhaps A K of a suit bid by dummy or declarer. It is usually not difficult for the opening leader to judge what lead is wanted. One example:

South	West	North	East
	1 ♦	2 ♣	2 ♠
Pass	4 ♠	Pass	6 ♠
Pass	Pass	Double	Pass
Pass	Pass		

South holds: ♠ 8 6   ♥ J 7 2   ♦ 9 7 5 3 2   ♣ 10 7 2

The double warns South not to lead clubs, the suit North has bid, not to make the neutral lead of a trump, and not to lead the unbid suit, hearts. Clearly the request is for a diamond. Probably North is void.

It follows that the player sitting over dummy should not double a slam when he wants his partner to make the natural lead.

We add with some diffidence that the principle of the Lightner double is often extended by good players to game contracts. Take this sequence:

South	West	North	East
1 ♣	1 ◇	1 ♠	Pass
3 ♠	Pass	4 ♠	Pass
Pass	Double	Pass	Pass
Pass			

A player who makes a simple overcall of One Diamond can hardly have a dynamic double of an opposing Four Spades. The presumption is that he wants his partner to lead a heart or a club, not the obvious diamond. This is a somewhat risky game to play in defence, but the reward is high when the coveted lead beats the contract.

SUMMARY

A redouble at part-score level is S O S when it is evident that the player cannot be strong enough for a business redouble.

An immediate cue bid in the opponent's suit is forcing until a suit has been supported. A deferred cue bid is a forward-going move, asking for further information.

When a bid of No Trumps can hardly be genuine it denotes distributional strength in the two lowest-ranking unbid suits.

A double of a No Trump contract means 'Lead our suit' or 'Lead a suit bid by dummy'.

The Lightner slam double asks for an unexpected lead.

CHAPTER 13

More about Competitive Bidding

How far to push – When to sacrifice – Psychology –
Doubling a high contract – Summary

MOST bridge players are either creepers or leapers, stone-
wallers or gay adventurers. This last group will get into the
bidding on the slightest excuse and will press on to the
uttermost in search of a fit. When they run into a misfit
hand or a bad trump break, they crash. Even so, we would
rather have our money on them than on an underbidder.
The adventurous player's good results tend to be spectacu-
larly good. Sometimes when he is already far out of his
depth the opponents will jump in and 'save' him.

The ideal, naturally, is to mix aggression with discretion.
A good bidder is alway thinking, 'How do our hands fit?
And what about the opponents – will the hand play well for
them?' The answer tells him when to advance and when to
draw back.

HOW FAR TO PUSH

How do you judge whether two hands fit well? Here is a
hand with two features that are very common. With East-
West vulnerable the bidding goes:

South	West	North	East
	1 ♣	Pass	1 ♠
2 ♡	3 ♠	4 ♡	4 ♠
?			

South holds: ♠ 8 5 3   ♡ K Q 9 6 5 2   ◇ A   ♣ 7 4 2

Four Spades will surely be made and Five Hearts is equally sure to cost something. Before reading further, can you identify the two features (apart from the obvious assets) that favour a sacrifice?

The first is your holding of three small cards in the suit the opponents have bid and supported. It is reasonable to suppose that partner will be short, so you should make two tricks by ruffing in his hand. (It is true that partner will have raised to some extent on the basis of his shortage, but he could not tell that it would be so useful.) The second good feature is that you have only low cards in clubs, the suit bid on your left, so any high cards your partner has in this suit will be working well. So, you sacrifice in Five Hearts; but if opponents go to Five Spades, take your chance on beating them. To drive the opposition to Five of a major is always an achievement.

Now let's look at the opposite situation. With neither side vulnerable the bidding goes:

South	West	North	East
1 ♣	1 ♦	1 ♡	1 ♠
3 ♡	3 ♠	Pass	Pass
?			

South holds: ♠ Q J ♡ A K 9 7 ◇ K 8 ♣ K J 7 3 2

All the signs are that this is a miracle fit – for the opponents. The spade holding is inauspicious and the King of diamonds is under the diamond bidder. If you drive the opponents to Four Spades they may make it, contrary to their own expectation. Although your side holds the balance of points you should let the bidding die in Three Spades.

WHEN TO SACRIFICE

There is, of course, a mathematical side to sacrifice bidding. In most situations a penalty of 500 to save a game is fair trading. With both sides vulnerable a paper loss of 500 shows a profit in real terms.

Below the game level you should not be too depressed to lose 300 to avert a part score. The real loss is not serious. With both sides vulnerable a loss of 200 to save a part score is good business.

Many players misunderstand the principles that govern sacrifice bidding when one side or the other has a part score. When your side has 60 below you should fight hard to defend it, for you are in a favourable position. When opponents have the part score you should be reluctant to pay heavily to prevent them converting it, for if they take a penalty from you they will retain their advantage. For some unexplained reason most players construe this in the opposite sense: they don't defend their own part score with any vigour, but they fight like tigers to prevent their opponents from clinching a battle that is already half lost.

There are some general portents in favour of a sacrifice which are a better guide than any attempt at exact analysis. These are propitious circumstances:

(1) It seems certain that the opponents will make their contract.

(2) You yourself don't expect to be more than 500 down.

(3) There is a chance that the opponents will attempt a higher contract instead of doubling you.

(4) Even if your other assets are somewhat nebulous, at least you hold a strong trump suit in the combined hands.

(5) You have 'shape', with singletons and voids rather than doubletons.

(6) You have reason to expect a fit – for example, that partner will be short in a suit where you have losers.

Still in very general terms, these are circumstances that are not propitious to a sacrifice:

(1) There is a definite chance, albeit slender, that you may defeat their contract. Bear in mind that odd values such as J x in an unbid suit, or a singleton King or Queen in the trump suit, sometimes mature into a trick when partner has a bolster in the same place. A 'phantom sacrifice', where

you lose points in saving against a non-existent game, is humiliating and expensive.

(2) The trump holding is not secure. The telling factor here is that by sacrificing you give opponents the option to double when they hold trump tricks and to outbid you when they don't. A bad trump division may lead to a very big penalty when opponents hold the balance of strength.

(3) You have a relatively flat distribution, such as 5-4-2-2 or 6-3-2-2.

(4) A sacrifice would involve taking a decision in front of your partner. He may hold unexpected defensive prospects.

(5) On a slightly different plane, the rubber is going badly, or you and your partner lack rapport. In either case, let the rubber go and start afresh.

Now for some hands that illustrate these points. With the opponents vulnerable the bidding goes:

South	West	North	East
1 ♠	2 ♢	3 ♠	4 ♢
4 ♠	?		

West holds: (1) ♠ 8 4 2   ♡ 6   ♢ A Q J 7 5 2   ♣ Q J 9

Bid Five Diamonds. The three low spades, as we noted in an earlier example, recommend a sacrifice. Five Diamonds cannot be expensive and there is the further point that if you can drive the opponents one higher you may well defeat them.

Now suppose that after the same bidding sequence West holds:

(2) ♠ 4   ♡ J 8 5   ♢ K Q J 8 6   ♣ Q J 8 3

This time West should pass. The singleton spade may coincide with a doubleton in partner's hand. Furthermore, West appears to hold little defence against a Five-level contract, so a bid of Five Diamonds will offer the enemy a soft option. As East still has a chance to speak, the decision should be left to him.

In the next example West has overcalled at the level of One.

South	West	North	East
1 ♡	1 ♠	2 ♡	2 ♠
4 ♡	?		

West holds: (1) ♠ K Q J 7 4 2   ♡ 5   ◇ Q 9 7 6   ♣ 5 3

West's hand is weak in defence, strong in attack. A bid of Four Spades in front of partner will convey this message. If the opponents contest further, the final decision can be left to partner.

After the same bidding sequence West holds:

(2)   ♠ K 9 7 4 2   ♡ 8 5   ◇ A Q 8 6   ♣ Q 3

Now there are two good reasons for passing: the trump situation may be insecure and Four Spades may be a 'phantom'. It all depends on the sort of hand that East has raised on.

PSYCHOLOGY

Despite Ely Culbertson's well-known saying that the only people who play bridge worse than professors of mathematics are professors of psychology, there is a place in bridge for the shrewd psychological stroke, especially in the field of competitive bidding. In the majority of competitive situations your opponents will take your bidding at face value and for the most part they will be right. However, this trust will also enable you to bluff them occasionally. There are three particular manoeuvres that are none the less effective for being well known. They are the bounce, the advance sacrifice, and the deliberate underbid.

(1) *The bounce.* North-South are vulnerable and the bidding goes:

South	West	North	East
1 ♠	2 ♦	2 ♠	3 ♦
?			

South holds: ♠ A K Q 7 6   ♡ 8 4   ♦ Q J 9   ♣ Q 6 3

Clearly South is hardly worth a competitive bid of Three
Spades, let alone a constructive effort. Nevertheless, if he
jumps to Four Spades the opponents may have no way of
knowing this. The deliberate overbid may cause the non-
vulnerable opponents to take a phantom sacrifice in Five
Diamonds. The safety factor in this manoeuvre is the strong
trump suit: lacking trump tricks, and suspicious of distributional storms, the opponents will not be able to double Four
Spades. The outcome may be one or two down un-doubled,
or may be a penalty conjured out of thin air against
Five Diamonds doubled.

(2) *The advance sacrifice.* With East-West vulnerable the
bidding goes:

South	West	North	East
	1 ♠	2 ♦	2 ♡
?			

South holds: ♠ 4   ♡ K 7 6   ♦ K J 8 5 3   ♣ 10 5 4 2

As South you expect to sacrifice eventually against Four
Hearts or Four Spades. It is good tactics to jump to Five
Diamonds at once. The opponents may settle on the wrong
suit or they may double prematurely. They may even pass!

(3) *The deliberate underbid.* North-South are vulnerable
and the bidding goes:

South	West	North	East
		1 ♠	2 ♣
?			

South holds: ♠ Q 10 7 6 3   ♡ 5 4   ♦ A 8 6 4 3 2   ♣ —

As South, you are worth a raise to game in spades, but this will prompt the opponents to sacrifice cheaply in Five Clubs. Play it cool, bid simply Two Spades! This way, you may gain the contract eventually in Four or Five Spades doubled.

Opportunities for tactical underbids of this sort may occur for the opening bidder as well as for responder, and also for the defenders. Another stratagem, holding excellent support for partner, is to bid a suit where your holding is very moderate, such as Q x x x or x x x. Thinking that their strength in this suit will prove a defensive asset, the opponents may be trapped into a premature double of the real suit.

DOUBLING A HIGH CONTRACT

We have already considered low-level penalty doubles in Chapter Nine. Doubles of high contracts are much less tentative, in the sense that partner will take it out only if he has misrepresented his hand. That is the test, as an example will show.

South	West	North	East
3 ♣	3 ♡	Pass	3 ♠
Pass	4 ♠	Double	Pass
?			

South holds: ♠ 8   ♡ 7 2   ◇ 5 4   ♣ K Q J 8 7 5 4 2

South could hardly hold a worse hand defensively, yet he should pass the double as his hand conforms to his previous bidding. This is North's party.

There is a big difference between a double of a freely bid contract, when there has been no competitive bidding, and a double after a competitive auction. The first point to note is that mathematically the odds are heavily against penalty doubles of high contracts: if you simply hope they have got one too high, don't double!

Against sound opponents who have reached a voluntary contract, it is not enough to hold an apparently strong hand. The time to double is when your hand contains an unpleasant surprise for the opponents. Two Aces against a slam do not qualify under this heading: it is charitable to assume that opponents know about Aces and that one of them has a void. In the same way, to double a confidently bid Four Hearts on an Ace-King and two Kings is a very flat-footed move. On the other hand, it may be right to double with Q J 9 x of trumps and a singleton of a suit bid by the dummy. This last item is an asset because it suggests that declarer will run into bad breaks.

In a competitive auction different considerations apply. As a rule, one side – not necessarily the opening side – is making the pace, the other is defending. When yours is the stronger side, bid up to your limit and double a sacrifice even if you cannot see the necessary defensive tricks in your own hand. When you are not optimistic about making a higher contract do not be afraid to double, if only to discourage partner from making any further advance. With North-South vulnerable the bidding goes:

South	West	North	East
1 ♡	1 ♠	4 ♡	4 ♠
?			

South holds: ♠ A 2   ♡ A 10 7 5 2   ◇ K Q 7   ♣ 8 6 5

South has three defensive tricks but many losers in a heart contract. He should signify this by doubling instead of letting Four Spades run up to his partner. North will be able to tell from his own hand that the double is not based on stacked trumps; he is free to bid on if he believes he can make Five Hearts.

SUMMARY

When considering a sacrifice, study whether there seems to be a fit (a) for your side, (b) for the opponents.

Holding the weaker cards – but a sound trump suit – contest vigorously even though you may suffer a fair-sized penalty if you are doubled.

When it is clear that your side will have to sacrifice eventually, be ready to bid the limit in advance.

After a non-competitive auction double only when your hand contains an unpleasant surprise for the opposition.

After a competitive auction be ready to double when you have bid as high as you can in your own suit.

Part Three

The Elements of Card Play

CHAPTER 14

Card Sense

*Establishing cards – Card placing – Choosing
between two plays*

MOST players admit there are things they can learn about
bidding, if only the eccentricities of experts. But when it
comes to play, they are more doubtful. 'Surely that depends
on experience and natural card sense,' they say.

Of course we do not deny the existence of card sense. It is
as real as a sense of humour or a sense of direction, and like
those it cannot be defined in terms of anything else. We do
not deny that there are some players – not many, even in
the ranks of experts – who have a remarkable flair for card
play. What we do say is that card sense is not difficult to
cultivate.

Many players who are now experts began as quite dull
performers and have improved through intelligent application. Knowledge of the numerous technical manoeuvres in
bridge is useful, certainly. But far more important is to have
a clear picture of the fundamentals. Card sense will come
automatically if you develop three basic skills. These are:

1. *Establishing cards*. On most deals you will start out with
not enough winners to make your contract. You will have
to establish some cards that are not winners. Your chances of
establishing enough winners may depend on how the opponents' cards are placed.

2. *Card placing*. On many deals it will be right to assume
that certain cards are placed where you want them to be, even
though there may be no grounds for thinking that they are so
placed. It will always be sound to 'place' cards if it will help

your line of play when you are right and will not cost when you are wrong.

3. *Choosing between two plays.* There may be more than one way in which you can establish enough tricks for contract. To make the correct choice you need to know a few simple rules about the ways in which cards are mathematically likely to divide.

We now outline the principles of establishment, card placing and choice of play. In time you will apply them automatically to every hand you play. At first we advise you to tackle each hand in the way that seems most natural at the time. Afterwards, look back on your play and see how far you have succeeded in applying the correct principles. Every time you spot a mistake you will greatly diminish the likelihood of making the same mistake in future. By a kind of geological process, your eventual skill will derive from the remains of the innumerable hands you have butchered in the past.

ESTABLISHING CARDS

We assume you know the mechanics of the simple finesse, know that you should not lead an unsupported high card, that you should always try to lead from the weak hand towards the strong hand, and so on. Here are some tips that follow on from there:

Play first the honours in the shorter hand. This will be more convenient in terms of entries and will also produce the maximum number of tricks.

(1)	*Dummy*	(2)	*Dummy*
	K Q 5		Q 6
	Declarer		*Declarer*
	A J 7 2		K 8 4 3 2

In the first example you should cash dummy's honours first, as dummy is the short hand. Nothing can stop you taking four tricks straight off. If instead you cash an honour

in the closed hand you will be at a disadvantage if the suit
does not divide 3–3. You will have to waste an entry later in
an outside suit in order to reach the closed hand.

In the second example declarer should lead a low card
towards the Queen in dummy, as that is the short hand. If
the Queen wins, declarer can duck the next round, gaining
when the hand on the left has A x. If declarer initiates the
suit by leading small and winning with the King, the Queen
is certain to be captured by the Ace on the next round.

Finesse the lowest card in a combination of honours. This is
specially important when cards are not in sequence. For
example:

	(1)	*Dummy*	(2)	*Dummy*
		A Q 9		K 10 5
		Declarer		*Declarer*
		6 4 3		7 4 2

In the first example declarer starts by leading towards
dummy's 9, and this play will establish a trick when the
Jack and 10 are well placed. If the 9 loses to the Jack or
10 on declarer's right, the Queen can be finessed when
declarer recovers the lead. This sequence of play is not
reversible: if the Queen is finessed first time, it will be too
late to play for the J 10 to lie under the A 9.

In the second example, if declarer starts by leading
towards the 10 he will make a trick if either the Q J or the
Ace are on his left. If he starts by leading to the King,
losing to the Ace, it will not help him later to find the Q J
well placed.

The same principle of finessing the lowest honour first
holds good with many other combinations. A finesse of the
9 from A J 9 is more likely to yield a trick eventually than a
finesse of the Jack. A finesse of the 10 from Q 10 x is more
likely to produce a trick than the play of the Queen. Almost
the only time when it is right to play a high honour is when it
is in sequence with another high card.

(1)	*Dummy*	(2)	*Dummy*
	K Q 10		Q J 9
	Declarer		*Declarer*
	7 3 2		6 4 2

It is correct to play up to the King in the first example and up to the Queen in the second. Only if declarer were short of entries to his own hand, and so unable to lead twice, would he take the deep finesse on the first round.

Do not lead an honour unless it is part of a strong sequence. Many tricks are lost by leading an honour on the first round in situations like this:

(1)	*Dummy*	(2)	*Dummy*
	A 6 2		A Q 10 6
	Declarer		*Declarer*
	Q J 5 4		J 5 4

In (1), if your objective is to make three tricks you should cash the Ace and lead towards the Q J x. If the Queen wins, re-enter dummy in another suit and lead to the J x. (If you are at all short of entries to the dummy it makes little difference to begin with a low card from the table towards the Q J x x.) You win three tricks whenever the suit is 3-3 and whenever East holds the King. Here you are simply following the familiar principle of leading towards honours rather than leading the high card itself. Many players would make the mistake of leading the Queen from hand. This costs when the player on the left holds x x and the player on the right K 10 x x and also when K x is on the right.

In (2), players tend to lead the Jack. If this is covered by the King from K x they lost the fourth round unnecessarily to the player who began with 9 x x x. Given time, the correct play is low to the 10. If this holds, re-enter the closed hand and finesse the Queen. This gains when the player on the left holds either K x or singleton King. It is correct to lead an unsupported honour in this type of situation only when a strong sequence is held, so that you can afford a cover. If in this example you held A Q 10 9 in dummy you could lead the Jack.

Play to develop long cards before you cash high cards. Few contracts can be made with the help of high cards alone. You will almost always need to develop some long cards – that is, low cards that become winners after the other hands have been exhausted of the suit. The development of long cards is always in the forefront of declarer's strategy, and generally it is right to establish long cards before cashing the top tricks. For example:

(1)   *Dummy*   (2)   *Dummy*
       A 8 4 3   9 6 4 3
       Declarer   *Declarer*
       K 6 2   A 8 2

In (1) you hope dummy's fourth card will become a winner. As you cannot avoid losing a trick en route, the correct play is to duck the first round. When you regain the lead you can cash the Ace and King, and if the suit fails to break you can go about your business elsewhere. To start by playing off Ace, King and another would leave the opponents on play to cash a fourth round in the event of a 4-2 break. Even if the suit is 3-3 you will need to waste an entry to reach dummy before you can enjoy the long card.

In (2) it would be still more uncouth to cash the Ace and lead another. Keep maximum control by ducking both the first and second rounds. You hope for 3-3, but you mentally place them 4-2.

CARD PLACING

Except when the tricks are there on top you will usually have to base your play on the assumption, or in the hope, that certain cards are placed in a certain way. Two principles apply:

If the contract seems safe, 'place' the cards in a manner that may endanger the contract. However bright the sun, expect rain. Assume the worst distribution that will still leave you with a chance for the contract. That is the basis of 'safety play'. Here is a simple example:

Declarer	Dummy
♠ A 2	♠ K 7
♡ 10 6 5	♡ A Q 7 3
◊ K Q 10 5 3	◊ A 2
♣ K 9 6	♣ A 8 3

You are in Three No Trumps and a spade is led. You have eight tricks on top and it is easy to begin cheerfully with Ace of diamonds and diamond to the King. That's wrong: consider first how bad a lie you can endure in the red suits. If there are five diamonds to the Jack, sitting over the declarer, and the heart finesse is wrong, it may be impossible to develop a ninth trick in time. But a simple safety play will take care of five diamonds on the other side. Win the spade opening, cash ◊ A and lead ◊ 2 from dummy. If next hand plays small, finesse the 10; if it loses to the Jack the fifth diamond will be good.

Equally often, the odds will seem to be against your making the contract. Then the second principle applies.

If the contract seems unsafe, 'place' the cards in a favourable way that will enable you to succeed. If possible, you should figure out a reasonably likely distribution that will give you a chance. In extreme cases you may need to assume a quite unlikely distribution. For example:

Declarer	Dummy
♠ K 10	♠ Q 6
♡ A K 7	♡ Q 4 3
◊ K J 10 9 7	◊ Q 5 3
♣ 8 6 5	♣ A Q 7 4 3 2

You are in Three No Trumps and a spade is led. Your nakedness is revealed when the Ace wins and the King and Queen fall together on the next round. Now, which suit to tackle? Of course, it is not difficult if you think about it. If you play on diamonds you will assuredly lose at least four spade tricks and the Ace of diamonds. Your only hope here is to run six club tricks. This involves finding K x under the dummy, a twenty per cent chance, for a 2-2 break is a forty per cent chance and half the time the King will be in the wrong hand. That sort of calculation brings us to the next section.

CHOOSING BETWEEN TWO PLAYS

In the play of most hands, especially at No Trumps, you will have a choice between various lines of play, between different suits to establish. To make the right choice, some knowledge of probabilities is essential. It is not necessary to remember exact figures, but you do need to remember the highlights.

With two cards against you, say the King and a small card, the odds very slightly favour playing for the drop; but there will often be indications pointing to a finesse.

With three cards against you, it is seven to two on their being 2-1 rather than 3-0. When you are missing K x x don't try to drop a singleton King: it is well against the odds.

With four cards against you, a 3-1 break is slightly more likely than 2-2. That does not mean, however, that missing Q x x x you should always finesse. Other things being equal, it is better to play for the drop.

With five cards against you, a 3-2 break is more than two to one on. This has great importance in practical play. When you have K J x x x opposite A x x, the odds favour a finesse for the Queen.

With six cards against you, a 4-2 break is distinctly more likely than 3-3. However, with K Q 10 x x opposite A x it is mathematically better to play for the drop than to finesse for the Jack. Another point: if both opponents follow to the first two rounds, the chance of 3-3 improves.

With seven cards against you, a 4-3 break is twice as likely as 5-2.

There is another group of probabilities, short but important, relating to finesses.

A simple finesse for a Queen or a King is obviously a fifty per cent chance, barring special indications.

A double finesse where you need two cards to be right for you is three to one against. But it is three to one on that one of the two will be right.

Dummy
A Q 10
Declarer
7 4 2

A finesse of the 10 will win only if both King and Jack are well placed. However, you will make two tricks with this combination three times in four, assuming you take two finesses.

A combination finesse, where you need one of two cards to be in a certain hand, is also three to one on.

Dummy
A J 10
Declarer
7 4 2

By taking two finesses you make two tricks except when both King and Queen are wrong. Thus you are three to one on. A slightly surprising, but in practical play highly significant, fact is that after the first finesse has lost to the King or Queen the second finesse is appreciably better than evens. (If this balks you, the explanation is that when an opponent wins with, say, the King there is an indirect assumption that he does not hold the Queen, for with K Q he might have played differently.)

We conclude with a couple of examples showing how the play is determined by understanding of these odds.

Declarer	Dummy
♠ A Q 6	♠ K 8 5
♡ K 6	♡ A 7
◇ 10 9 7	◇ K J 8 4 2
♣ 8 7 6 4 2	♣ K Q J

You are in Three No Trumps and a heart is led. You can afford to lose the lead only once again, so you must decide whether to play on diamonds or clubs. To make four tricks in diamonds you will need to find the Queen favourably placed, a fifty per cent chance. You can make four tricks in clubs if they break 3-2, and that, as we have noted above, is more than two to one on. So the best chance is to force out the Ace of clubs.

The next example is a little more complicated.

Declarer	Dummy
♠ A K 6 2	♠ Q J
♡ 9 4	♡ A K 10 8
◇ A 7 3	◇ Q 6 5 2
♣ A Q J 10	♣ K 4 2

You are in Six No Trumps and after a spade lead you can see eleven tricks on top. Where will you go for the twelfth?

One possibility is to find the King of diamonds in front of the Queen. You don't play the Ace first, because if this play fails you don't want to give the opposition a chance to cash the setting trick in diamonds before you have tested the hearts. If you have no luck with the diamonds you will need to find both Queen and Jack of hearts in front of the A K 10 8.

To find the King of diamonds right is a fifty per cent chance. If that fails, you have one chance in four of making the extra trick in hearts. Of the fifty cases remaining after the Queen of diamonds has lost to the King, you will salvage a trick in hearts just over twelve times. Combined chance; about sixty-two and a half per cent.

Is there anything better? Surely! Take the combination finesse in hearts, running the 9 and, if that loses, finessing the 10 on the next round. This is a seventy-five per cent chance. And before you take the second finesse you may as well lay down the Ace of diamonds, on the off chance that the King may be single. Only a three per cent chance, but many people have made fortunes with less than that going for them!

CHAPTER 15

Forming a Plan of Attack

*Count of winners – Attacking the danger hand – The
plan in a suit contract – The ruffing game – Reverse
dummy play*

LIKE the military men who are always happy to find an
excuse for a roll-call, you must, when the dummy goes
down, count your top tricks and also the tricks that can be
quickly established. The very best players do that on every
hand, so you don't want to be the odd man out.

COUNT OF WINNERS

After counting the winners, and possible winners, you note
the dangers. When you have established a relation between
the two, you have a plan. Let's look at a few hands that you
might play in Three No Trumps.

♠ K 7 4 2
♡ 10 9 5 4
♢ A 8
♣ A 10 3

♢ 5 led

```
    N
  W   E
    S
```

♠ A 8 5 3
♡ Q J
♢ K J 6
♣ K J 9 2

Before you play from dummy you assess the prospects. The certain tricks are three diamonds, two spades and two clubs. Given time, it must be possible to establish two tricks in hearts, a third trick in clubs, and probably a third trick in spades.

As you need to set up two extra tricks for game it is not difficult to see that you should play on hearts. You are a 'tempo' ahead of the defence, for you can knock out the Ace and King of hearts before they can cash any long diamonds.

Now let's change the hand slightly, depriving the declarer of one of his diamond tricks.

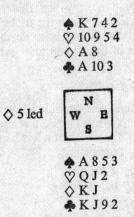

```
                    ♠ K 7 4 2
                    ♡ 10 9 5 4
                    ◇ A 8
                    ♣ A 10 3

                      ┌─────┐
                      │  N  │
   ◇ 5 led           │W   E│
                      │  S  │
                      └─────┘

                    ♠ A 8 5 3
                    ♡ Q J 2
                    ◇ K J
                    ♣ K J 9 2
```

Now you have only six tricks on top. To play on hearts (*a*) will not produce the required three tricks and (*b*) will be too slow, for the opponents will take at least three diamond tricks and two hearts before you can enjoy the long hearts. To make the contract you will need some luck in both black suits. First, you cross to dummy with ♣ A and run the 10 of clubs. If this loses and the opponents continue diamonds you will be two down, but if the club finesse holds you have a good chance. After taking four club tricks you duck a round of spades. That may produce game by way of three spades, four clubs and two diamonds.

ATTACKING THE DANGER HAND

On many hands the plan depends on which opponent you regard as the danger hand. Again you are in Three No Trumps with:

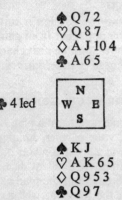

♠ Q 7 2
♡ Q 8 7
◊ A J 10 4
♣ A 6 5

♣ 4 led

♠ K J
♡ A K 6 5
◊ Q 9 5 3
♣ Q 9 7

You are going to play low from dummy on the club lead, so you defer full planning until East has produced ♣ J and you have won with the Queen.

You have six top winners in the form of three hearts, a diamond and two clubs. A 3-3 heart break would provide an extra trick, but there is no hurry to test that. By forcing out ♠ A you can develop two spade tricks. A successful finesse in diamonds would by itself produce enough tricks for the contract.

Up to now it seems logical to play on the diamonds. However, there is a tactical aspect to be considered. Suppose the diamond finesse loses and the clubs are cleared. Now you cannot be sure of a ninth trick, for the hearts may not break and when you play a spade West may be able to win and cash enough clubs to beat the contract.

The solution is to play first the suit where the dangerous opponent, West, may hold an entry. At trick 2 you lead a spade. If opponents take the Ace and clear the clubs you will be able to take the diamond finesse with safety later in the play. Suppose, alternatively, that the Jack of spades is allowed to win. In that case you hastily turn to diamonds, with nine tricks guaranteed. To play a second spade would be an unnecessary risk, for East might hold ♠ A 10 x x x x and the King of diamonds.

Sometimes it is necessary to develop a suit in a special way to stop the dangerous opponent from gaining the lead. We give some examples of that in the next chapter. First, we study the general planning in a suit contract.

THE PLAN IN A SUIT CONTRACT

Once again, the ground rule is to form a plan before playing a card from dummy. (If your partner, holding a singleton of the suit led, attempts to play it for you on the opening lead, restore it to the dummy with silent disapproval.) The nature of the plan is different from the plan at No Trumps, for now you must count the losers as well as the winners. The losers tend to determine the line of play. That is clearly seen in the following hand, played in diamonds.

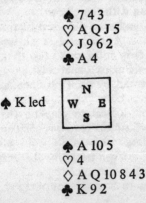

```
                    ♠ 7 4 3
                    ♡ A Q J 5
                    ◇ J 9 6 2
                    ♣ A 4

                   ┌─────────┐
                   │    N    │
   ♠ K led         │  W   E  │
                   │    S    │
                   └─────────┘

                    ♠ A 10 5
                    ♡ 4
                    ◇ A Q 10 8 4 3
                    ♣ K 9 2
```

Before reading further, see if you can form a plan to make (1) Four Diamonds, (2) Five Diamonds, (3) Six Diamonds, and (4) Seven Diamonds.

1. *Four Diamonds*. You can afford to lose two spades and a trump. Simply win with the Ace of spades, cross to the Ace of hearts, and run the 9 of diamonds. If this loses to the King the defenders will cash two spades, but that will be all.

2. *Five Diamonds*. Now you want to improve on the simple chance of the diamond finesse being right. One possibility is to take an immediate finesse of the Queen of hearts. If it wins, you can discard a spade on the Ace of hearts and lose at most one spade and one diamond. The disadvantage of this play is that you might lose the King of hearts and two spades while the diamond finesse was right all the time. You are not really improving your chance – you are just taking the heart finesse instead of the diamond finesse.

A better line is to take a ruffing finesse in hearts. After capturing the first spade you cross to dummy with ♡ A and return the Queen. If East covers, you ruff and lay down the Ace of diamonds. If the King does not fall, you cross to ♣ A and lead the Jack of hearts, discarding a spade, Barring accidents, you will lose only one diamond and one spade. And if East does not cover the Queen of hearts? Then you discard a spade. West may win and cash a spade. but you still have the diamond finesse in reserve. You are favourite to make Five Diamonds whenever East holds one of the red Kings.

3. *Six Diamonds*. Now you need a little luck. You begin by finessing the Queen of hearts. If it wins, you cash the Ace and lead a third round, ruffing with ♢ 8. You may bring down the King of hearts in three rounds, and in that case you can cash the Ace of diamonds and later throw your second spade on the established Jack of hearts. If you fail to bring down the King of hearts you will need the diamond finesse (a distinctly better chance than bringing down the singleton King).

4. *Seven Diamonds*. There are two ways of setting about

this contract. One way is to follow the same line as when you were trying to make Six. If you can win the heart finesse and bring down the King in three rounds you will have two discards for the spades. If the diamond finesse is right too, you make the contract.

The other method (though such play is rather outside the scope of this book) is to play for a squeeze. You win with ♠ A, cross to ♣ A, and pick up the trumps. After ruffing the third round of clubs you lead off all the trumps. Now if West began with ♠ K Q J and ♡ K he will be squeezed on the last diamond. If he reduces to ♡ K x and ♠ Q, dummy's ♡ A Q J will take the last three tricks.

Apart from being an amusing exercise, this hand shows how important it is to count the losers and form a comprehensive plan at the beginning of the play.

THE RUFFING GAME

When you set out to play a trump contract you should always focus your attention on one point: 'Do I draw trumps, or not?'

In general, it is right to draw trumps unless there is a clearly defined reason for not doing so. We saw on the last hand that in some variations trump leads were postponed to give declarer a chance to discard losers. The trump element comes into its own when declarer aims to make his trumps separately. On the next hand it is obvious that declarer may want to take ruffs on the table, but he mustn't be too precipitous.

                    ♠ 8 5 3 2
                    ♡ K 10 7
                    ◇ 4
                    ♣ K 9 7 5 2

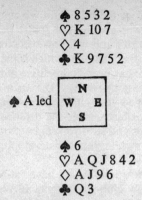

♠ A led

                    ♠ 6
                    ♡ A Q J 8 4 2
                    ◇ A J 9 6
                    ♣ Q 3

South plays in Five Hearts after competitive bidding.
West, who has overcalled in spades, leads the Ace and
follows with a low spade to his partner's King. You ruff
and consider your prospects.

Your first thought may be that by not leading a trump
at the second trick the defenders have given you a chance to
ruff three diamonds on the table. There is a snag in this
which you may not see at first. Suppose you lead Ace of
diamonds at trick 3 and continue with a cross-ruff. You will
arrive at this position, with the lead in dummy:

                    ♠ —
                    ♡ —
                    ◇ —
                    ♣ K 9 7 5 2

                    N
                 W   E
                    S

                    ♠ —
                    ♡ A Q J
                    ◇ —
                    ♣ Q 3

You play a club from the table and whichever defender holds the Ace will win and play a spade or a diamond. You will be forced to ruff and will now be defeated if either opponent began with three trumps, which is highly probable on a hand where there has been competitive bidding.

So, where have you gone wrong? The answer is that you ought to have developed your club trick earlier in the hand.

But that, you may object, gives the defence a chance to lead a round of trumps and stop you ruffing three diamonds. So it does, but meanwhile you are developing a threat in another direction.

The best play at trick 3, after you have ruffed the second spade, is to lead a low club from hand. If West holds the Ace he will already have a problem, for if he ducks you will switch to a cross-ruff game, and if he goes up with the Ace he lets you make the King and Queen separately. In that case, you will probably be able to establish a long club as well.

The worst that can happen when you lead the low club is that East will head the King with the Ace and return a trump. Probably your best chance now is to play for the clubs to be 3-3. You win the trump return, cash ♣ Q, cross to dummy with a trump and ruff a low club, hoping the suit will divide.

You may say: 'I see, after the full analysis, that attempting to take three diamond ruffs is likely to fail in the end; but how would I work that out in advance without taking too long?'

The answer is that, as in most situations, you can rely on general principles. When you need tricks from a side suit as well as from a cross-ruff, it is always right to play for the side tricks first. If you fail to do this the defenders will have a chance to discard while the cross-ruff is in progress and it may be impossible later to enjoy the side winners.

The usual procedure in a trump contract is to take ruffs in the short hand – usually the dummy – and draw trumps with the long hand. Sometimes that process is reversed, as in the next example.

REVERSE DUMMY PLAY

Hands, like faces, may look different when you see them the other way up. In a suit contract it is always worthwhile to consider whether you should make dummy the master hand, or your own. That is to say, will you take ruffs in the dummy and draw trumps from your own hand, or the other way round? Here the contract was a grand slam:

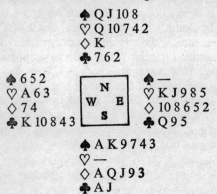

♠ Q J 10 8
♡ Q 10 7 4 2
◇ K
♣ 7 6 2

♠ 6 5 2
♡ A 6 3
◇ 7 4
♣ K 10 8 4 3

♠ —
♡ K J 9 8 5
◇ 10 8 6 5 2
♣ Q 9 5

♠ A K 9 7 4 3
♡ —
◇ A Q J 9 3
♣ A J

The bidding went:

South	North
2 ♣	2 ◇
2 ♠	3 ♠
4 ◇	5 ◇
7 ♠	Pass

The opening Two Clubs was conventional and North's raise to Three Spades on the next round left room for the exchange of information. When South bid a second suit North raised to show a control. This was just what South wanted to hear.

West, determined not to look foolish, led the Ace of hearts. South quickly dissipated the effect of the good bidding. He ruffed the heart, drew three rounds of trumps, cashed ◇ K, and returned to hand with ♣ A. He was able to discard dummy's club losers and ruff a club, but as the diamonds did not break he was left with a losing diamond and no more trumps on the table.

This is a hand that should have been played 'upside down'. After the heart lead South should treat the dummy as the master hand. He plays a low trump to dummy at trick 2, ruffs another heart, crosses to ◇ K and ruffs a third heart. Dummy is entered once again in spades and a fourth heart is ruffed by South's last trump. Now the 9 of diamonds is ruffed, the outstanding trump is drawn, and the rest of South's hand is high, his losing club having been discarded on dummy's fourth trump.

It is not necessary on this type of hand to project the play trick by trick. South should see at once that he can ruff hearts four times. Thus he will take, in effect, eight tricks in the trump suit. That is better than making six trumps in his own hand plus one ruff on the table.

CHAPTER 16

Communications

Hold-up play – Shutting out the long suit – Duck Soup

To be at the right place at the right time is one of the main arts of card play. For the declarer there may be two objectives: one is to maintain good communications for his own side, the other to spike the enemy guns. To keep the entries fluid, to be able to take the finesses you want, is in most cases just a matter of looking ahead. One general principle worth bearing in mind is that early tricks should usually be taken in the hand opposite the long suit you plan to develop. This is a fairly simple example:

```
                    ♠ A K 9 3
                    ♡ K 7 4
                    ◇ A J 5
                    ♣ A 8 6
                    ┌─────────┐
                    │    N    │
    ◇ 4 led         │ W     E │
                    │    S    │
                    └─────────┘
                    ♠ 7 5
                    ♡ Q J 8 6 2
                    ◇ K 8
                    ♣ J 7 4 2
```

The bidding goes:

South	West	North	East
		1 ♠	Pass
1 NT	Pass	3 NT	Pass
Pass	Pass		

South responds One No Trump because he lacks the minimum of 9 points for a response at the Two level. North, with 19 opposite a minimum of 6, ventures a game bid.

West leads a low diamond and the critical play occurs at trick 1. If South puts in the Jack of diamonds, taking a 'free finesse', East may produce the Queen. South can hold up the King, but another diamond will be returned. Now South is in danger of being cut off from his good hearts, for if either defender holds ♡ A x x he will hold up the Ace until the third round.

The play is quite easy so long as South goes up with the Ace of diamonds on the first trick, keeping the King as an entry for the long hearts. At trick 2 declarer leads a low heart to the Queen, then a heart back to the King. Unless the hearts are 4-1 declarer will make four tricks in hearts and he has five top winners in the other suits.

HOLD-UP PLAY

We noticed in the last example that a defender who held ♡ A x x would hold up his Ace until the third round. That kind of play is frequently used by the declarer, as on the following hand:

♠ A 10 6
♡ 7 4
◇ K J 4 3
♣ A 7 6 2

♡ 5 led

```
      N
   W     E
      S
```

♠ K 5
♡ A J 6
◇ A 8 7 5 2
♣ K 5 3

South opens One Diamond, North raises to Three Diamonds, and South bids Three No Trumps. West leads the 5 of hearts and East plays the King.

Unless all four diamonds are in East's hand South has enough tricks for game by way of four diamonds and five winners in the other suits. However, there is a danger, for one of the defenders, probably West, may hold five hearts. In that case, unless the diamonds are solid, south may find himself losing four hearts and a diamond.

The normal antidote is to hold up the heart Ace for as long as possible. South plays low on the first round and East leads back the 9. Now the Jack loses to the Queen and a heart is returned, on which East plays the 3.

The play strongly suggests that West began with five hearts and East with three. (If East held four hearts it would be normal to return the fourth best at trick 2, to help his partner count the suit.) South lays down the Ace of diamonds and leads a second diamond on which West plays the 10. With nine cards originally, the odds slightly favour playing for the drop, but there is a tactical reason why that would be the wrong play now. South does not mind losing the lead to East but cannot risk losing a trick to West, who probably has two hearts to cash. South takes a safety finesse of the Jack, therefore. Whether this wins or loses, the contract will be safe unless he has completely misjudged the lie of the hearts.

When declarer has only one winner in the suit led it is right to hold up unless a switch to another suit is still more to be feared. He has more of a problem when he holds the King and Queen, either in the same hand or in opposite hands.

```
              ♠ 9 5 2
              ♡ Q 10 7 4
              ◇ K 6 5
              ♣ A K J

                  N
♠ 6 led      W         E
                  S

              ♠ K Q 4
              ♡ A J 8
              ◇ A 9 4
              ♣ Q 9 5 3
```

South opens One No Trump and North raises to Three No Trumps. West leads the 6 of spades, dummy plays low, and East produces the Jack. Sometimes it is right to hold up with K Q x, but not here, because the critical play will be the finesse in hearts towards West. South should win with ♠ K, cross to dummy with a club, and run the 10 of hearts. If the finesse loses, West cannot continue spades to any good purpose.

Now let's change the hand slightly, giving South the King of hearts instead of the Ace.

```
              ♠ 9 5 2
              ♡ Q 10 7 4
              ◇ K 6 5
              ♣ A K J

                  N
♠ 6 led      W         E
                  S

              ♠ K Q 4
              ♡ K J 8
              ◇ A 9 4
              ♣ Q 9 5 3
```

Again the 6 of spades is led and East puts in the Jack.
The play at trick 1 depends on your estimate of who holds
the Ace of hearts. If West, then obviously you should play
the King of spades; but if East holds the Ace of hearts
together with J x of spades it will be a mistake to win, for
when he comes in with ♡ A he will lead a spade and West
will make four tricks in the suit.

You cannot be sure who holds the Ace of hearts, but in
the absence of any other indication it is reasonable to assume
that the Aces are divided. On the whole, it is better play to
duck on the first trick. Note that if East holds three spades
and the Ace of hearts the contract is safe anyway, for you
will lose at most three spades and ♡ A.

The problem is the same in effect when the King and
Queen are in opposite hands.

♣ Q 5

6 led

♣ K 7 3

West, who has overcalled in clubs, leads the 6. Again the
right play depends on which opponent you expect to win the
first defensive trick. If you will be finessing towards West
then it will be right to go up with the Queen; but if the first
finesse will be towards East, the best play may be to duck
in both hands.

Here is another combination that should be treated in
the same way:

J 7

A 10 8 5 3 2   Q 6

K 9 4

When West leads the 5 and East plays the Queen, hold up
the King. Then if West has no side entry you will shut out
his suit.

A declarer holding Q J x x may be tempted to part with
his control too soon. Suppose the distribution to be:

6

A 10 7 5 3   K 9 4

Q J 8 2

East plays the King on the first lead and returns the 9.
Now South would be wrong to cover. If he puts in the Jack,
West will duck and take the rest of the tricks as soon as
East is able to lead the suit again. In the diagram position
an expert East might play the 9 on the opening lead. If
South can read this position he should duck as before.

SHUTTING OUT THE LONG SUIT

Has it struck you that there are many holdings where the
best communication play is to go up with an honour on the
first round? These are the 'blocking' plays.

A 8 6

6 led

J 7 3

You will be taking a finesse in West's direction later and
you want to avoid losing four tricks in the suit led. The best
chance is to go up with the Ace, blocking the suit when East
began with K x or Q x. True, the play of the Ace will be a
mistake if West has led from K Q x x x, but that is less
likely.

Here are two other situations where the play of the
Ace will usually stop the opponents from running four quick
tricks:

(1) A 5   (2) A J

10 7 6 2   9 8 5 3

When West leads a low card in (1) you may assume that
East holds one of the three missing honours. If West is
likely to hold the first side entry you can block the run of
four tricks by going up with the Ace. Similarly, with (2)
the play of the Ace on the first trick blocks the run when East
hold Q x or K x.

Perhaps the most important of all the plays of this class occurs when West leads a suit bid by his partner and the distribution is like this:

$$
\begin{array}{c}
7\,4 \\
Q\,8\,6 \qquad\qquad A\,10\,5\,3\,2 \\
K\,J\,9
\end{array}
$$

West leads the 6 to his partner's Ace and East returns the 3, his original fourth best. Now the King will block the run of the suit. It is true that West might have led the 6 from 10 8 6, but East's play of the Ace is significant, for with A Q x x x he would normally put in the Queen.

One group of communication plays belongs more to the defence than to the attack. This is a well-known position:

$$
\begin{array}{c}
A\,J\,9\,6\,3 \\
K\,10\,7 \qquad\qquad Q\,8\,4 \\
5\,2
\end{array}
$$

Suppose that South leads the 2 towards a dummy that is short of entries. If West plays low and the 9 fetches the Queen, the declarer will take four tricks in the suit when later he finesses the Jack. By withholding his Queen East can hold the declarer to two tricks, but better still is for West to put up the King on the first round. That play would be equally right with, for example, Q x x in front of dummy's A J 10 x x.

For some reason this type of play is often missed when declarer has the opportunity for the same blocking play.

$$
\begin{array}{c}
Q\,10\,5 \\
8\,2 \qquad\qquad A\,J\,9\,6\,3 \\
K\,7\,4
\end{array}
$$

When West leads the 8, his partner having bid this suit, declarer should go up with the Queen in dummy. If East ducks he gives South a second trick, and if he plays the Ace he cannot return the suit without giving South two tricks.

DUCK SOUP

The declarer's main weapon for establishing his own long suits is the familiar ducking play. The play appears here in its simplest form:

A K 8 5 3

6 2

Even if dummy has no side entry South may be able to establish and run four tricks by ducking on the first round.

When a specific number of tricks is needed it may be right to duck even when there is a chance to take all the tricks, as with this combination.

A Q 8 4 3

K 7 5

Needing four tricks, South leads the King and then, if West follows suit and dummy lacks entries, he ducks the second round. This gains when the distribution is 4-1. Note that the same play may be required when North holds A J x x x and West Q 10 x x.

Much less obvious are the occasions when a deep duck is advisable.

♠ A 5
♡ A Q J 8 4
◇ 7 4 2
♣ 8 6 3

♠ J 9 4   ♠ Q 10 8 6 2
♡ 7 3 N ♡ K 10 9 5
◇ Q 8 6 3 W E ◇ J 10
♣ J 10 9 7 S ♣ K 4

♠ K 7 3
♡ 6 2
◇ A K 9 5
♣ A Q 5 2

West leads ♣ J against Three No Trumps, East plays the

King, and South wins, as he does not want a switch to spades at this point. Suppose that declarer makes the normal play now of finessing ♡ Q. If East knows his way round the table he will duck. South returns to hand for another heart finesse, but this time East wins and switches to spades. The long hearts in dummy are now shut out for lack of entries.

Needing precisely three tricks from hearts, declarer should duck on the first round, letting East win with the 9. He takes the spade return with the King and finesses ♡ Q. This loses, but the remaining hearts in dummy are good and the Ace of spades is an entry.

The same sort of 'deep duck' may be required when declarer has K Q J x x opposite x x, or simply K Q x x x opposite x x, with one sure entry on the table.

Here is a deal where the declarer may need to duck in two suits at just the right moment:

```
                    ♠ K 9 6 3
                    ♡ 10 7 2
                    ◇ K 5
                    ♣ A Q 6 2
   ♠ 10 5              ┌─────┐        ♠ 8 4 2
   ♡ A Q J 3           │  N  │        ♡ 9 5 4
   ◇ Q J 9 3         W │     │ E      ◇ A 10 7 4
   ♣ K 10 4            │  S  │        ♣ J 8 5
                      └─────┘
                    ♠ A Q J 7
                    ♡ K 8 6
                    ◇ 8 6 2
                    ♣ 9 7 3
```

The bidding goes:

South	West	North	East
Pass	1 ♡	Pass	Pass
1 ♠	Pass	2 ♠	Pass
Pass	Pass		

The North-South hands do not fit well and accurate play is required even for Two Spades. When West leads $\Diamond$ Q South has the opportunity for his first mistake. Suppose he covers with the King – a pointless and in this case misguided manoeuvre. East will win and return the 9 of hearts to his partner's Queen. West may be sufficiently inspired now to underlead his Jack of diamonds in the hope of putting his partner in the lead again; then another heart from East will give the defence five tricks in the red suits, with a club to follow.

To restrict entries to the East hand, South should play low from dummy on the Queen of diamonds lead. West plays a second diamond to his partner's Ace. East returns $\heartsuit$ 9, making it clear he has no higher card, West wins and exits with a trump.

To avoid losing three heart tricks South must develop a long card in clubs, at the same time keeping East out of the lead. When he wins the first trump he leads a club to dummy's Queen. He comes back to hand with a second trump and leads another club. Now if West plays the King it is allowed to hold, and if he plays low he is thrown in on the third round. A third diamond is ruffed in dummy, the King of spades draws the outstanding trump, and the thirteenth club is good for a heart discard.

South has avoided two pitfalls in the play. The first was when he refused to cover the Queen of diamonds at trick 1. The second mistake he could easily have made would have been to cash the Ace of clubs when in dummy; this would have given West a chance to unblock by throwing the King of clubs under the Ace.

There was a third opportunity to go wrong which you may not have noticed. If he draws a third trump earlier on, South gives a clever West the chance to discard the King of clubs and create a certain entry to his partner's hand.

CHAPTER 17

Defence

> *The lead against No Trumps – The lead against a
> suit contract – Planning the defence – Inferences
> from the lead – Note declarer's first line of attack –
> Finding the right discards – A switch in time*

DEFENCE begins with the opening lead, a difficult subject
and one where players are ill-served by many of the old
textbooks, not to mention some modern ones. We advise you
to disregard those 'tables of preferred leads' which begin
with A K Q at the top and have villains like K J x at the
bottom of the list. The opening lead is a tactical problem to
be considered in the light of the bidding and the make-up
of your hand. We begin with the lead against No Trumps,
rather simpler than the lead against a suit.

THE LEAD AGAINST NO TRUMPS

The general rule, as doubtless you know, is to attack from
length. The opponents reach Three No Trumps after a
confident auction, no suit being mentioned, and you hold:

♠ 7 3 2   ♡ A Q 6   ◇ K 9 7 5 2   ♣ Q 10

It would be foolish to consider any lead but a low diamond. The conventional lead is the fourth best, the 5 in this
instance. You know it may give a trick away, but this need
not be the ninth trick and anyway you must hope that
partner has some length in diamonds. To play for partner's
hand, say by leading ♠ 7, would be a mistake because it is
extremely unlikely that he will have enough entries to
establish his length.

When you have a weak hand yourself there may be a better case for opening a suit where you hope to find your partner at home. As West you hold:

♠ Q 6 3   ♡ 10 6 4   ◇ J 8 7 4 2   ♣ 9 8

If the bidding has been simply One No Trump–Three No Trumps, you may as well try the diamonds. To play any other suit is a long shot, for you have no indication where partner's strength may lie. But suppose North, on your left, has opened One Heart and has rebid the suit over Two No Trumps. Now, with a certainty of a long suit against you, it becomes urgent to find a dynamic defence. It is unlikely that you will be able to accomplish anything in time with your diamonds. If you decide to play for partner's hand, which suit will you lead – a spade or a club? Clubs offer the better chance because, you must remember, your partner did not overcall with One Spade, as he might have done with length in spades and a fair hand.

When you have no five-card suit. The choice is always critical when you hold only four-card suits. The bidding against you has been One No Trump–Three No Trumps and you have to lead from:

♠ 8 7 2   ♡ K J 7 6   ◇ K 8 4 3   ♣ 7 6

The 8 of spades is a safe lead that won't give anything away, and you may find partner with some length. However, the lead does not appeal greatly because the opponents may have reserves of strength and it may therefore be essential to get a suit going at once. Best is to lead a heart, despite the possibility that you may be playing up to declarer's A Q.

However, if the contract of Three No Trumps had been reached in more halting fashion, or if you had been defending against One No Trump or Two No Trumps, there would be much better grounds for making a safe, neutral lead such as ♠ 8. It might be one of those hands where the defence should sit back and let declarer take all the finesses.

The conventional leads. Having established that the lead is

determined by tactical considerations, not by comparing
the holding in one suit with another, we can turn to the
choice of card when you have settled on a particular suit.
The general rule is to lead the higher of touching honours
when you hold three, and otherwise the fourth best from a
long suit. We look now at a few holdings where the general
rule does not necessarily supply the answer.

A K x x x

From five or six cards headed by A K lead fourth best;
but from A K x x lead the King and judge whether or not
to continue when you have seen the play to the first trick.

A Q 10 x x

Here the choice depends on whether you hold a sure side
entry. If so, lead the Ace and judge the continuation when
you see the dummy. With no quick entry outside, lead
fourth best.

A 10 9 x   K 10 9 x   Q 10 9 x x

From a four-card suit lead the 10 – the higher from an
interior sequence. From five cards lead low if you think that
declarer may hold four cards; otherwise lead the 10.

K Q 9 x   Q J 9 x x   J 10 8 x x

In each case lead the top card.

K x x   Q x x   J x x   10 x x

With all these holdings lead low, whether or not partner
has bid the suit. It may be important to keep an honour over
the declarer. For example, to lead the King from K x x
costs a trick when partner has Q 10 9 x and declarer A J x.

9 6 4 2   8 6 4

From four cards, lead low if you aim to develop a long
card; but if you are leading the suit more for safety, choose
a middle card. From three cards the highest tends to be
clearest. Against a suit contract, as we shall see, it is com-
moner nowadays to lead the middle card.

THE LEAD AGAINST A SUIT CONTRACT

It is a fair generalization to say that the lead against No Trumps is based on the time factor, the lead against a suit on safety. At No Trumps you are willing to surrender a trick when you open a long suit because you expect to develop low cards later. In a suit contract there may be no advantage in developing low cards, so for the most part the object is to avoid giving a trick away by the lead.

Safe leads. When you hold touching honours, lead one of the honours, not a low card.

A K x x   K Q x x x   Q J x x x

From a suit headed by A K it is conventional to lead the King. From the other two holdings lead the top card.

K x x   Q x x x   J x x x

The lead from a single honour is seldom attractive unless there is reason to suppose that partner has strength in the suit. Of the three combinations, the lead from the Jack is the least safe and the least likely to achieve anything.

K x x x x   Q x x x x   J x x x x

As the length increases, the lead becomes safer, in that it is unlikely to give up a vital trick. The lead from J x x x x is now as safe as from the other combinations.

9 7 5 3

This type of lead is unlikely to give anything away. A middle card should be led, so that partner can see there are no tricks to develop.

9 7 5

The modern style is to lead the middle card and follow with the highest. This tells partner you have three and not a doubleton.

Short suit leads. A lead from a plain singleton or doubleton is relatively safe and contains an element of aggression in that it may lead to a ruff.

The lead from a doubleton is seldom a first choice, for it may help declarer to develop the suit and the prospect of a ruff is usually remote. There is more to recommend the lead when the player holds a trump trick. For example, you have to lead against Four Hearts, no other suit having been mentioned, from:

♠ 7 3   ♡ K 10 5   ◇ A 8 6 4   ♣ J 8 6 2

The 7 of spades is certainly best here. If partner holds the Ace and no side entry he should duck the first trick so that you can lead a second spade when you come in with the King of hearts. Neither of the alternatives looks attractive. The lead from an unsupported Ace often costs a trick, whether you lead the Ace or, deceptively, a low card.

Attacking leads. When it is apparent from the bidding that the opponents hold one or more side suits it may be good policy to make an attacking lead, such as low from K x x or Q x x, the Queen from Q x, the Ace from A x, even the King from K x.

Another type of attacking lead is fourth best from a long suit when you hope to weaken the declarer's trump position. Suppose the contract is Four Spades and you have to lead from:

♠ 10 7 4 2   ♡ K J 8 5 3   ◇ 9 4   ♣ A 6

Unless it is clear that both opponents hold at least four spades, the best plan may be to attack the declarer by leading hearts. If you can force him to ruff either now or later you may end up with the long trump. A forcing lead, as this is called, is always a powerful defence when it comes off.

Trump leads. Finally, there are times when a trump is a good lead. Sometimes it is chosen for safety, because any other lead may give up a trick, sometimes for a more purposive reason. Suppose the declarer has shown length in two suits and has been supported in one of them: then a trump lead may prevent him from obtaining ruffs in the side suit. When the trump suit has been strongly supported there are always grounds for expecting the declarer to play a ruffing game and a trump opening may well be the best defence.

We have said enough to show that to make the killing lead you must listen to, and interpret, the bidding. The player who wakes from slumber and says, 'What's the contract? Is it my lead?' is unlikely to find a dynamic opening.

PLANNING THE DEFENCE

We will not attempt to cover the technique of defence in a few pages. We *will* try to set you thinking on the right lines.

A declarer forms a plan when he sees the dummy. This is not so easy for the defenders, who have not the advantage of seeing two hands in combination. The defensive drill should go something like this:

1. Whether declarer plays quickly or slowly from the table at trick 1, make an assessment before you play a card.

2. Study dummy's holding and relate it to the bidding. Is the dummy stronger or weaker than might have been expected? Does it look as though the declarer will have an easy time unless the cards are such and such, or is it the sort of hand where the object of the defence should be to give nothing away?

3. Coming to details, what do you suppose partner holds in the suit he has led? Why has he led this suit? What does it tell you about his holding in the other suits?

4. How much do you know at this point about the declarer's hand?

5. Where are the defensive tricks coming from?

All that, you see, is rather different from the declarer's count of winners and losers. The defenders can seldom count winners and losers at an early stage.

INFERENCES FROM THE LEAD

Some inferences from the lead will be obvious, some less so. If partner leads a plain card higher than the 7 it is quite likely that he holds no high honour. If he begins with a low card against No Trumps you assume he is leading fourth best from his longest suit. Those are obvious inferences.

One train of thought leads to another. Against No Trumps, if partner leads the 2, or any other card which is plainly the lowest from a four-card suit, you can form an opinion about his holdings in the other suits, which he has deemed less attractive.

In a suit contract partner fails to lead the suit you have bid. A possible reason is that he holds four or five cards and does not see any possibility of setting up tricks in this department. Another possibility is that he has a holding such as A x and does not want to take the risk of opening up the suit in case declarer has the King.

After competitive bidding where your side has bid one suit strongly and this seems the natural lead, partner leads a low card of another suit. This is probably a singleton.

It is particularly important at No Trumps to form an estimate of partner's length in the suit he opens. If he leads the 3 and the 2 is not in sight, perhaps he holds four and perhaps five. Watch carefully to see what he plays on the next round.

NOTE DECLARER'S FIRST LINE OF ATTACK

Much can be deduced from the declarer's play when he first gains the lead. At No Trumps he will generally play the suit where he needs to develop tricks. A clear inference arises when he fails to play on a long suit held by the dummy or rebid by himself. Almost always it means that he has the missing 'tops', for otherwise he would be developing this suit. You should construct his holding on that assumption, and often the conclusion will be that you must make a dramatic assault in another direction.

In a suit contract the declarer's first line of play always tells a lot about his hand. Broadly speaking, there are four types of play in a suit contract, and to each the defenders have a natural antidote. The four types are:

1. *The ruffing game*, where declarer plays for an early ruff on the table. The defenders must study whether, by trump leads, they can frustrate this.

2. *The cross-ruff game*, where declarer aims to ruff in both hands. Now the defenders must lead trumps even though they may be losing a trick in the trump suit itself; for example, a defender must not hesitate to broach trumps from a holding such as Q x x.

3. *The no-trump game*, where declarer draws trumps and plays to establish side winners. On this type of hand the defenders do best to avoid opening up new suits.

4. *The suit-establishment game*, where declarer's aim is to set up a suit in dummy by ruffing and then to draw trumps. The best defence now may be to force the dummy to ruff so that declarer cannot draw trumps and return to the table to cash the winners in the long suit. If that defence doesn't look promising it may be necessary to look for quick tricks in another department.

FINDING THE RIGHT DISCARDS

One of the most difficult parts of defence is to discard well when declarer leads off a long suit, usually the trump suit. It is very important now to use length-showing discards. A defender who discards from a five-card suit begins with his lowest card, but from an even number he plays high-low. This helps each defender to count the declarer's hand. This is more useful than playing high-low to signal strength.

An inference that should never be missed occurs when the declarer in a trump contract makes no attempt to ruff a side suit in dummy. The presumption is that he has no losers to ruff. Suppose this is the dummy in a high spade contract:

♠ Q 9 6 3   ♡ A 8 4   ◇ K 3   ♣ J 9 6 3

The declarer wins the first trick in hearts or clubs and plays off several rounds of trumps. Now it is a certainty that he has no losing diamonds to ruff – he may hold a

doubleton or A Q x, but not A x x. The defenders can let this
suit go with confidence, yet in such situations you will
often see a player hanging on to a guarded Jack or Queen
and discarding his real prizes.

A SWITCH IN TIME

In the 'defensive drill' we outlined earlier in this chapter, the
last question was: 'Where are the defensive tricks coming
from?' The critical moment in most contracts occurs after
the first or second trick and at this point the defenders must
try to form a constructive plan of some sort.

As a rule, the game at No Trumps is to persevere with the
suit originally led, but quite often an alert defender can see
that he must go elsewhere for tricks. This type of hand is
very common:

```
                    ♠ J 6
                    ♡ J 9 7 5 2
                    ◇ J 6 4
                    ♣ A 10 8

  ♠ 10 8 7 5 3      ┌─────┐      ♠ K Q 4
  ♡ K 6 3           │  N  │      ♡ Q 10 4
  ◇ 9 7 2         W │     │ E    ◇ A 5
  ♣ 7 5             │  S  │      ♣ J 9 6 4 3
                    └─────┘
                    ♠ A 9 2
                    ♡ A 8
                    ◇ K Q 10 8 3
                    ♣ K Q 2
```

The bidding goes:

South	North
1 ◇	1 ♡
2 N T	3 N T
Pass	

North's raise to Three No Trumps is borderline but not
wrong. West leads his fourth best spade and East holds the

first two tricks with ♠ Q (lowest card from a sequence) and ♠ K. South must hold off because the defenders threaten to take four spades and the Ace of diamonds.

When his partner drops the 3 on the second round of spades, East realizes that he began with five. But will it help to clear the spades? Has West a re-entry, and in what suit?

If West has an entry in diamonds, the contract can be defeated even if a spade is not returned at this point. (When diamonds are led East, if his alternative plan has not succeeded, can go up with the Ace and lead his third spade.) But suppose West's entry is in hearts, and the King rather than the Ace? In this case it may be essential to attack hearts at once.

It is not very likely that declarer has ♡ A K x, so East is not taking a great risk when he leads a low heart at trick 3. If declarer passes this, West wins with the King and returns a heart. The defenders now win two spades, two hearts and the Ace of diamonds.

It is clear that if East unimaginatively plays a third round of spades, declarer will win four diamond tricks, three clubs and two Aces. A switch in time saves nine.

Part Four

The Finer Points

CHAPTER 18

The Standard Coups

*The throw-in – Elimination play – Avoidance
play – Loser on loser – Trump coups*

THERE are some sparkling manoeuvres in play which are
also big point-winners. They go by the general name of
'coups'. Most of them are not difficult to perform, once you
know the type and can recognize the opportunity. In these
examples we try to explain what you should be looking for.
All the coups are quite common in practical play.

THE THROW-IN

In this coup the declarer throws the lead to a defender who
is then forced to play up to a tenace combination. Throw-ins
occur most often in No Trump contracts. Here is a typical
end position:

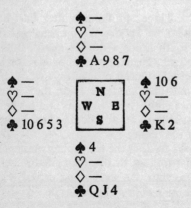

South needs two of the last three tricks. If he finesses the Queen of clubs he will lose a club and two spades. If instead he throws East in with a spade, then East must concede the last two tricks when he leads a club.

Sometimes the declarer knows a throw-in will succeed, sometimes he is merely hopeful. On the following hand he can make a pretty good guess about the lie of the cards.

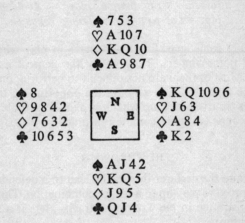

♠ 7 5 3
♡ A 10 7
♦ K Q 10
♣ A 9 8 7

♠ 8
♡ 9 8 4 2
♦ 7 6 3 2
♣ 10 6 5 3

♠ K Q 10 9 6
♡ J 6 3
♦ A 8 4
♣ K 2

♠ A J 4 2
♡ K Q 5
♦ J 9 5
♣ Q J 4

South plays in Three No Trumps after East has opened the bidding with One Spade. West opens ♠ 8 and East, knowing that South holds a double guard, puts in the 9, won by South's Jack. The Ace of diamonds is forced out and East leads King and Queen of spades.

South wins the third spade, keeping the 4 as a possible exit card. He has eight tricks in sight and his general plan is to throw East in the lead at a point where he will have to play clubs into the tenace.

The first step is to cash the remaining winners in the red suits. When East follows to three rounds of each red suit, South places him with two spades and probably two clubs. He has reached the position shown in the first diagram. He exits with a spade, as planned, and after cashing two spades East has to lead a club away from the King.

The throw-in on the last hand was not a complete certainty to succeed, for East might possibly have held only one club and the thirteenth card of one of the red suits. (It *would* be a certainty if West had previously discarded a heart and a diamond.) Many throw-ins are foolproof, like the next example.

♠ 7 6 4 3
♡ K 10 6
◇ J 7
♣ Q 9 5 4

♠ 5 led

```
  N
W   E
  S
```

♠ A K 2
♡ A J 5
◇ Q 8 4
♣ K J 10 2

South is in Two No Trumps and a spade is led. South wins and forces out the Ace of clubs. The defenders play a second spade, both following suit. South wins and cashes a second and third, but not a fourth club. Then he exits with the 2 of spades.

Let us suppose that West began with four spades and cashes two winners. On the fourth spade South discards his last club. Now West is obliged to open up one of the red suits, giving declarer his eighth trick without any risk.

There was one quite subtle point in the play of this hand, which you may not have noticed. If declarer cashes *all* the clubs before exiting with ♠ 2, he himself has an awkward discard on the last spade. He can throw a heart, but then the defence can exit in hearts and declarer is in trouble with entries.

ELIMINATION PLAY

When the defenders lead a suit which can be ruffed by the declarer in either hand, his own or dummy's, they are said to concede a ruff and discard. It will generally cost them a trick. When declarer brings about a situation where the defenders are forced to give up a trick either by conceding a ruff and discard or by leading into a tenace, he is said to perform 'elimination play'.

Eliminations are more common than throw-ins and are also easier to execute, for usually there is no risk at all – just a good chance, or a certainty, of success.

You should always watch for an elimination when you have superfluous trumps in each hand and a tenace holding in another suit. The procedure then is to eliminate from the defending hands any cards they can safely play when thrown in. Here is a situation you will meet many times:

```
              ♠ A Q 7 5 2
              ♡ 9 4
              ◇ A 10 6
              ♣ 7 4 3

                 ┌─────────┐
                 │    N    │
♡ Q led          │ W     E │
                 │    S    │
                 └─────────┘

              ♠ K J 8 6 3
              ♡ A 5
              ◇ K Q 2
              ♣ K 10 2
```

South is in Four Spades and a heart is led. After declarer has won with the Ace nothing can defeat him, for he can draw the adverse trumps, eliminate the diamonds, and exit with a heart. Suppose, at worst, that ♣ A Q J is over the King. East wins the heart lead and plays a club; declarer puts in the 10 and after winning with the Jack West is 'on play', forced either to return a club or concede a ruff and discard.

When a declarer complains 'both finesses were wrong', as often as not he could have saved the ship by an elimination. The next example is a little deceptive – but quite easy if you know the type.

The contract is Four Hearts and a trump is led. The 'unlucky' player draws trumps, then finesses ♣ 9. This loses to the 10 and when West wins the next round of clubs he leads a diamond. Curtains!

How to make a certainty of this hand? Remember the idea is to make opponents open up a dangerous suit. After drawing trumps you discard a diamond in dummy on the third spade, then play Ace of diamonds, followed by Queen of diamonds. You don't care who has the King, for when the defenders win the second diamond they are in the classical dilemma, forced to open up the clubs or allow a ruff and discard.

```
                    ♠ A 9
                    ♡ J 6 4 2
                    ◇ A Q 2
                    ♣ Q 9 7 4

    ♠ J 8 6 4         N          ♠ 10 7 3 2
    ♡ 9 5                        ♡ 8 7
    ◇ J 9 7 6    W       E       ◇ K 10 4 3
    ♣ A 8 3           S          ♣ K 10 5

                    ♠ K Q 5
                    ♡ A K Q 10 3
                    ◇ 8 5
                    ♣ J 6 2
```

Sometimes the elimination play just gives an extra chance. On a hand like this you hope for a favourable distribution:

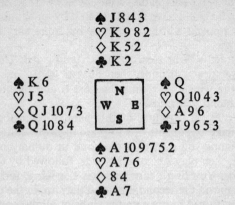

```
                    ♠ J 8 4 3
                    ♡ K 9 8 2
                    ◇ K 5 2
                    ♣ K 2
  ♠ K 6                            ♠ Q
  ♡ J 5                            ♡ Q 10 4 3
  ◇ Q J 10 7 3                     ◇ A 9 6
  ♣ Q 10 8 4                       ♣ J 9 6 5 3
                    ♠ A 10 9 7 5 2
                    ♡ A 7 6
                    ◇ 8 4
                    ♣ A 7
```

You are in Four Spades and the defence begins with three rounds of diamonds, obligingly disposing of that suit. You lay down the Ace of spades, cash two clubs and two hearts. Then you exit with a trump, hoping that the player who wins will not have a third heart to play. It costs nothing to try and the play succeeds.

There is enormous variety in elimination play. Remember to look for an elimination possibility whenever you have trumps to spare.

AVOIDANCE PLAY

This is another great stand-by. The idea is that, like a boxer slipping a punch, you avoid an untimely blow from an opponent's high card. This is the most characteristic form:

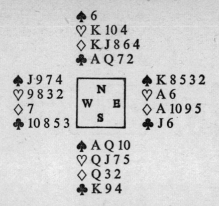

```
                    ♠ 6
                    ♡ K 10 4
                    ◇ K J 8 6 4
                    ♣ A Q 7 2
    ♠ J 9 7 4                      ♠ K 8 5 3 2
    ♡ 9 8 3 2          N           ♡ A 6
    ◇ 7            W       E       ◇ A 10 9 5
    ♣ 10 8 5 3         S           ♣ J 6
                    ♠ A Q 10
                    ♡ Q J 7 5
                    ◇ Q 3 2
                    ♣ K 9 4
```

South is in Three No Trumps and a spade is led to the King and Ace. If declarer follows a simple line, leading a diamond towards dummy at the second trick, he will be defeated, for East will return a spade through the A 10. With diamonds and clubs breaking badly, there will not be enough tricks for game. Nor will it avail South to force out ♡ A: East will win the first round and attack spades.

The winning play is to cross to dummy with a club at the second trick and lead a small diamond from the table. This is an avoidance play. If East goes up with the Ace, it will beat the air, leaving South with four diamond tricks. And South will not mind, of course, if West is able to capture this trick, as West cannot lead spades to any good purpose.

Whenever declarer needs to establish tricks in two suits he should consider the possible advantage of an avoidance play. That is the only way to make game on the following deal:

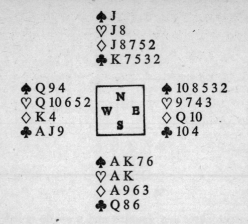

♠ J
♡ J 8
◇ J 8 7 5 2
♣ K 7 5 3 2

♠ Q 9 4   ♠ 10 8 5 3 2
♡ Q 10 6 5 2   ♡ 9 7 4 3
◇ K 4   ◇ Q 10
♣ A J 9   ♣ 10 4

♠ A K 7 6
♡ A K
◇ A 9 6 3
♣ Q 8 6

A heart is led against Three No Trumps. It is no use clearing the diamonds, for even if they break well, South will be a trick behind. The right play at trick 2 is a low club from hand. If West goes up with the Ace, declarer has four club tricks, and if West ducks, the King wins and South can turn to diamonds.

Many avoidance plays of a slightly different kind can be practised within the compass of a single suit. These are two combinations that are frequently misplayed:

   (1)   A Q x x   (2)   A J x x x
            J x   Q x

With (1) the best way to develop three tricks is to lead low away from the A Q. This gains when East holds K x or K x x. Similarly, with (2) the best play for four tricks is low from dummy. This gains when East has K x, for if East ducks, the Queen will win and declarer can duck or play the Ace on the next round.

Still another form of avoidance play was seen in the hand on page 165, where the object of the play was to prevent a particular opponent from gaining the lead. The situation was that shown in (1) below:

(1)   A Q x x   (2)   A Q J x x
   K 10 x   J x x   K x   10 9 x x
        x x x   x x

In each case declarer can develop the suit without letting
East into the lead. He plays from hand each time, intending
to duck if West plays the King. This type of play has
numerous variations.

LOSER ON LOSER

In this elegant manoeuvre the declarer trades a loser in one
suit for a loser in another. For example, instead of ruffing an
opponent's winner he allows it to hold, discarding a loser
from another suit. There are many ways of gaining a tactical
advantage by this play. Here the loser on loser prevents a
dangerous opponent from gaining the lead while a key suit
is being developed:

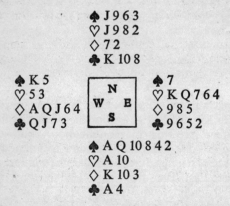

          ♠ J 9 6 3
          ♡ J 9 8 2
          ◇ 7 2
          ♣ K 10 8

♠ K 5   ♠ 7
♡ 5 3   **N**   ♡ K Q 7 6 4
◇ A Q J 6 4 **W** **E** ◇ 9 8 5
♣ Q J 7 3   **S**   ♣ 9 6 5 2

          ♠ A Q 10 8 4 2
          ♡ A 10
          ◇ K 10 3
          ♣ A 4

South plays in Four Spades after West has opened One
Diamond and East has responded One Heart. The 5 of
hearts is led and South heads the Queen with the Ace. Now
East is marked with ♡ K Q, so West must hold the rest of
the high cards. The Ace of spades fails to drop the King, so

the danger now is that East will gain the lead in hearts and play a diamond through the King.

South combats this threat by playing Ace and another club. Whether or not West splits his honours, South wins with ♣ K and returns the 10, discarding his losing 10 of hearts. This play prevents East from gaining the lead and also enables declarer to establish two heart tricks by means of a ruffing finesse through East's King.

Neat and simple, yet easy to miss if you don't know it, is a loser-on-loser play to avoid an overruff. On this next deal declarer needs to obtain two ruffs in the red suits.

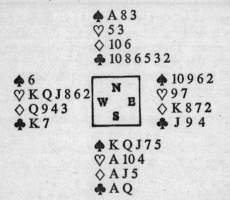

```
                    ♠ A 8 3
                    ♡ 5 3
                    ◇ 10 6
                    ♣ 10 8 6 5 3 2
    ♠ 6                             ♠ 10 9 6 2
    ♡ K Q J 8 6 2      N            ♡ 9 7
    ◇ Q 9 4 3       W     E         ◇ K 8 7 2
    ♣ K 7              S            ♣ J 9 4
                    ♠ K Q J 7 5
                    ♡ A 10 4
                    ◇ A J 5
                    ♣ A Q
```

South plays in Four Spades after West has overcalled in hearts. The King of hearts is allowed to win the first trick and declarer's Ace wins the continuation. South can manoeuvre to ruff one diamond with a low trump and a heart with the Ace of trumps, but in that case he will lose a trump eventually to East. The solution is to lead the third heart and discard a diamond from dummy. Then he can ruff two diamonds with low trumps.

TRUMP COUPS

There are a number of coups which may come to the declarer's rescue when straightforward play in the trump

suit will not succeed. Most of them involve a trump reduction, where declarer deliberately shortens his trump
holding by ruffing. Here is a bright little coup which saves
a guess in the trump suit:

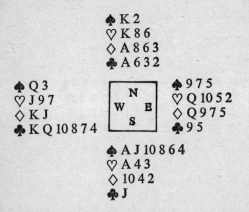

South is in Four Spades and West, who has overcalled in
clubs, leads the King. There are two diamonds and a heart
to lose, so the contract appears to depend on finding the
Queen of spades. There is no need to finesse, for a trump
reduction play removes all guesswork.

Declarer wins the club opening, ruffs a club, plays ♡ A
and ♡ K, then takes another club ruff. After a diamond to
the Ace he ruffs clubs for the third time, reducing his trumps
to A J 10. Now he simply exits with a diamond and must
make three more tricks. The play has the quality of a throw-
in as well as a trump coup.

Note that it was essential to make full use of dummy's
entries for the purpose of shortening trumps: the coup would
not have worked if South had not ruffed a club at trick 2.

It is often good technique to ruff as a routine measure, just
in case the trumps prove awkward. That precaution is
necessary on this deal:

Against South's contract of Four Spades the defenders
take three heart tricks and exit with a diamond. If declarer

plays Queen of spades and a spade to the Ace he will lose eventually to East's Jack. How does he avoid this without taking an unnatural finesse?

With commendable foresight he ruffs a diamond at

```
                    ♠ Q 3
                    ♡ 7 6 4
                    ◇ A 7 5 4 3
                    ♣ K 9 2

    ♠ 2              ┌─────────┐        ♠ J 9 6 4
    ♡ K J 8 5        │    N    │        ♡ A 10 9
    ◇ Q 10 8 2       │  W   E  │        ◇ K J 9
    ♣ 10 7 6 5       │    S    │        ♣ J 4 3
                     └─────────┘
                    ♠ A K 10 8 7 5
                    ♡ Q 3 2
                    ◇ 6
                    ♣ A Q 8
```

once, then leads Ace of spades and a spade to the Queen, discovering the bad break. Another diamond ruff produces the desired situation where declarer's trump length is the same as that of the defender. The position is:

```
                    ♠ —
                    ♡ —
                    ◇ 7 5
                    ♣ K 9 2

    ♠ —              ┌─────────┐        ♠ J 9
    ♡ —              │    N    │        ♡ —
    ◇ Q              │  W   E  │        ◇ —
    ♣ 10 7 6 5       │    S    │        ♣ J 4 3
                     └─────────┘
                    ♠ K 10
                    ♡ —
                    ◇ —
                    ♣ A Q 8
```

Declarer plays three rounds of clubs, ending in dummy, and makes the last two tricks with ♠ K 10.

In a final example declarer accomplishes the same sort of manoeuvre at the expense of his left-hand opponent.

```
                    ♠ 10 8 4 2
                    ♡ J 8 4
                    ◇ A Q 10
                    ♣ Q J 5
    ♠ Q J 9 6                      ♠ —
    ♡ 10 7 2      ┌─────────┐      ♡ A K 6 5 3
    ◇ 9 4 3       │    N    │      ◇ 7 6 5 2
    ♣ 10 6 4      │  W   E  │      ♣ 9 8 3 2
                  │    S    │
                  └─────────┘
                    ♠ A K 7 5 3
                    ♡ Q 9
                    ◇ K J 8
                    ♣ A K 7
```

South is in Four Spades and the defence begins with two rounds of hearts. East then switches to a club. Declarer lays down the Ace of spades and finds that he has two natural losers in the suit.

No need to despair! Declarer cashes two more rounds of clubs and three rounds of diamonds, hoping that West will follow suit. Then he leads the Jack of hearts and ruffs it. The fact that he is ruffing a winner gives this play the official dignity of a 'grand coup'. South exits with a small trump and West finds that one of his apparently certain trump tricks has vanished into the air!

CHAPTER 19

Count Your Way to Better Play

A complete count – A partial count – Counting in defence

WHEN does a card player really 'arrive'? Not when he executes his first squeeze or end-play, but when he first starts working out suit lengths in the unseen hands and applying the knowledge to get more out of the cards.

When he does this he becomes a different player. The whole process of card play becomes more accurate, as he is basing his operations on fifty-two cards instead of just the twenty-six he can see.

You may think we are exaggerating a little. It is true that on some hands the length of the various suits is less important than the position of the high cards. However, two examples will show that we are not pitching it too high.

(1)	*Dummy*	(2)	*Dummy*
	A J 6 3		A 5
	Declarer		*Declarer*
	K 10 9 5		K Q 10 6 2

In the first example you want to pick up the missing Queen. If you have no information about suit lengths you have only a fifty-fifty chance of guessing where the Queen lies.

Now suppose you have been able to work out the distribution of the unseen hands, technically known as 'getting the count'. We will say that East is marked with three cards of this suit, West with two. The odds are now three to two that East holds the Queen. Instead of an even guess you have odds of six to four in your favour.

In the second example the normal play would be to cash three top honours, hoping the Jack would fall. But if you have got a count and can place East with, say, four cards in this suit, it will be twice as likely that the Jack is with East rather than West. You should therefore finesse the 10 on the second round.

We give these examples only to show that knowledge of suit lengths is more valuable than one might think at first. There are many more ways in which counting the hand will help your game.

A COMPLETE COUNT

To get a count, let's face it, some work is needed. You have to keep track of the cards played in each suit and you have to form a picture of the thirteen cards dealt to an opponent.

Players have different methods of counting. It is not difficult for an experienced player to retain a mental image of each trick and to know almost instinctively how many cards of each suit have gone and how many are left. To reconstruct an opponent's hand demands more positive effort. The best way is to store up the inferences that can be drawn from each trick as it is played. When you do this, it is almost as though you were playing a different game. Deals that would have been humdrum before suddenly become exciting.

A player who counts will make his contract on the following deal, where another would be defeated and not even realize there was more to it than bad luck.

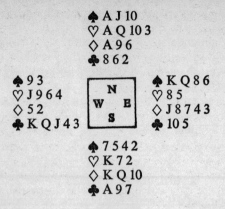

The contract is Three No Trumps and the King of clubs is led, followed by the Queen. You win the third round and East discards a diamond. There are eight certain tricks. The ninth must come from either spades or hearts.

The first move is to lead a spade and finesse the 10, which loses to the Queen. You win the diamond return and finesse ♠ J. This loses too and East plays back a third spade, on which West discards a club. The position is now:

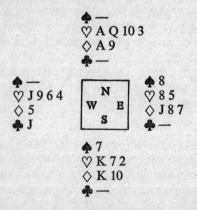

To make the contract you need four tricks from hearts.

Do you cash the three top honours or do you finesse the 10 on the first round?

Of course, it's easy when you can see all the cards (as players always say when justly rebuked by their partners). The interesting point is that if you play correctly you do, in all that matters, see all the cards.

So far you know that East began with four spades and two clubs. You cannot get a complete count until you know about three suits, so before tackling hearts you should play off the Ace and King of diamonds. As it happens, West shows out on the third round, discarding his last club. The contract is now icy, as East must hold precisely two hearts. After cashing the Ace and King you can finesse the 10 with complete confidence.

Although a 'show-out' in three suits is needed for a perfect count, a show-out in only two suits may suffice when the distribution of the third suit can be gauged from the bidding. For example:

```
                    ♠ Q J 10 7 6
                    ♡ A 9
                    ◇ A 9 6 2
                    ♣ 10 7
     ♠ 8 4                             ♠ 9 2
     ♡ Q J 10 2         N             ♡ 8 7 5
     ◇ 4            W       E         ◇ J 8 7 5 3
     ♣ A Q 8 5 3 2       S            ♣ 9 6 4
                    ♠ A K 5 3
                    ♡ K 6 4 3
                    ◇ K Q 10
                    ♣ K J
```

South opens One Spade and lands in Six Spades after West has overcalled with Two Clubs. The Queen of hearts is led and after winning with dummy's Ace declarer draws trumps in two rounds. As the Ace and Queen of clubs are likely to be with West, South needs to win four diamond tricks so that he can obtain a discard of his losing club.

So far declarer has a sure count of only one suit, the trumps. He gets a count of the hearts by playing ♡ K, heart ruff, diamond to the King, heart ruff. When East shows out on the fourth round West is marked with four hearts as well as two trumps.

Now South is almost there. West is unlikely to have overcalled on ♣ A Q x x x only, so is marked with six clubs. That leaves him with one diamond at most. In dummy after the second heart ruff, South finesses ◇ 10 and cashes the Queen. Then he crosses to dummy with a trump and parks a club on the Ace of diamonds.

When there is a fair amount of bidding it is often possible to form a picture of the likely distribution after one or two tricks. At No Trumps, particularly, the opening lead always tells a tale. If an opponent leads 'top of nothing' you have the inference that he did not care to lead from any of his long suits, and if he appears to be leading from length you can form an opinion about this length in the other suits. See how that works on the following deal.

```
                    ♠ A Q 7 2
                    ♡ A K 4
                    ◇ A 7 6 3
                    ♣ 6 5

    ♠ K 10 4                        ♠ 9 5 3
    ♡ 8 5          ┌───────┐        ♡ J 9 6 2
    ◇ Q 10 4 2     │   N   │        ◇ 8
    ♣ A 10 8 3     │ W   E │        ♣ J 9 7 4 2
                   │   S   │
                   └───────┘
                    ♠ J 8 6
                    ♡ Q 10 7 3
                    ◇ K J 9 5
                    ♣ K Q
```

North opens One Spade after two passes, South responds Two No Trumps and North raises to Three No Trumps. A low club is led, won by the King. Declarer doesn't know exactly how the clubs are divided but he does know he cannot afford to lose a trick anywhere. It seems natural to play on diamonds, for four diamond tricks will see him home. A diamond is led to the Ace, therefore, and on the return East discards a spade.

Now declarer needs six tricks from hearts and spades. He begins with a finesse of ♣ Q, which holds. If he then bangs out the top hearts he goes one down. The proper continuation is the Ace of spades, to gain more information about how this suit is dividing.

West follows with the 10 of spades and is known to have the King left. He has turned up with ◊ Q 10 x x and must have at least four clubs, as he led them. That leaves him with at most two hearts, and the play is an open book.

In the next example we observe the inference that can be drawn from a neutral lead.

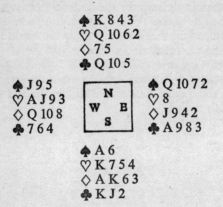

♠ K 8 4 3
♡ Q 10 6 2
◊ 7 5
♣ Q 10 5

♠ J 9 5
♡ A J 9 3
◊ Q 10 8
♣ 7 6 4

♠ Q 10 7 2
♡ 8
◊ J 9 4 2
♣ A 9 8 3

♠ A 6
♡ K 7 5 4
◊ A K 6 3
♣ K J 2

South opened One Heart and was raised to Two Hearts. He rebid Two No Trumps and North bid the game in No Trumps.

West led the 7 of clubs, the 10 was played from dummy, and East, reading the lead as highest of three, encouraged by playing the 8. A low heart was led to the King and Ace, and West led a second club. East completed his signal by dropping the 3 and South won in hand.

As soon as East played the 8 of clubs on his partner's lead of the 7, it registered on the declarer that West had apparently led a short suit, rather surprisingly in view of the bidding. Perhaps his only four-card suit was hearts?

When East completed his signal on the second round of clubs, South decided to play his hunch. He led a second heart from his own hand and successfully took the deep finesse of the 6. Though interesting as a piece of card-reading, this manoeuvre was not altogether necessary, for if the 10 of hearts is finessed East has an awkward discard: if he lets go a diamond or a spade he enables South to set up a winner in that suit.

A PARTIAL COUNT

It is comparatively rare for the declarer to have a complete count when he makes the critical play. As a rule, there are simply indications that have a bearing on the odds.

North-South reached Six Hearts and West led a low club, partly because clubs had not been mentioned and partly because it is often right to make an attacking lead against a small slam. East won with the Ace and returned a club, South ruffing.

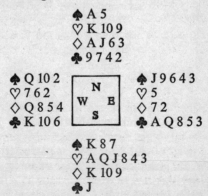

♠ A 5
♡ K 10 9
◇ A J 6 3
♣ 9 7 4 2

♠ Q 10 2   ♠ J 9 6 4 3
♡ 7 6 2   ♡ 5
◇ Q 8 5 4   ◇ 7 2
♣ K 10 6   ♣ A Q 8 5 3

♠ K 8 7
♡ A Q J 8 4 3
◇ K 10 9
♣ J

The contract depends on finding the Queen of diamonds

and the correct procedure now is to discover as much as possible about the opposing distribution. Declarer plays a heart to the 9 and ruffs another club, on which West's King appears. A heart is led to the 10, East throwing a spade. Three rounds of spades follow, producing this situation:

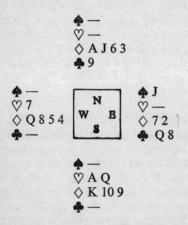

South places East with the Queen of clubs, as with K Q 10 West would have led a high club. There is no point in keeping the 9 of clubs as a threat card, so to settle the club distribution South ruffs a fourth round and West discards a diamond. Now the last trump is drawn and East discards his fifth club.

A lazy declarer would say to himself, 'East had a singleton heart, so I will play him for the long diamonds.' A more careful analysis establishes that East began with five clubs and at least four spades – probably five, for if West had held ♠ Q J 10 he might have led that suit rather than a club. Thus it is probably East who began with the short diamonds and the percentage play is to finesse against West.

When declarer has nine of a suit, missing the Queen, only a slight breeze is needed to incline him towards a finesse. This is a very common type of hand:

                         ♠ K 7 6 4
                         ♡ 8 2
                         ◇ A 9 5 3
                         ♣ Q 10 6

                         ┌─────────┐
                         │   N   │
    ♡ 5 led   W   │   E │
                         │   S   │
                         └─────────┘

                         ♠ A Q 2
                         ♡ Q J 3
                         ◇ K J 10 6 2
                         ♣ K 8

    South is in Three No Trumps. West leads ♡ 5, East wins with the Ace and returns the 9, on which South plays the Queen and West the 4.

    It looks very much as though West began with five hearts, so all depends on finding the Queen of diamonds. As West has two more hearts than his partner, the odds at this moment favour playing East for the Queen. However, before making the critical decision South should take three rounds of spades. If West turns up with four or even three spades, the odds will favour playing him for a singleton diamond. If West has two spades, then declarer may as well play for the drop in diamonds. If West has a singleton spade, then declarer should change plan to the extent of playing him for Q x x of diamonds.

COUNTING IN DEFENCE

Counting in defence has two sides to it. The more difficult side is forming a picture of the distribution round the table. This can be done only by careful signalling. In general, a player who is not making an encouraging or discouraging signal on his partner's lead should seek to convey his distribution by playing high-low with an even number of cards, the lowest with an odd number. In the trump suit it is conventional to play high-low with three trumps precisely.

The second type of counting is that of checking where the declarer's tricks are coming from. This is slightly easier in the sense that less information is required and there is less dependence on partner. Observe West's predicament on the following deal.

```
              ♠ Q 10 9 5
              ♡ A 10 9
              ◇ Q J 10 9
              ♣ 7 4
♠ K 6 2          N          ♠ J
♡ Q J 8 4    W     E       ♡ K 7 5 3
◇ K 6 2          S          ◇ 7 5 4
♣ A 8 3                     ♣ Q J 6 5 2
              ♠ A 8 7 4 3
              ♡ 6 2
              ◇ A 8 3
              ♣ K 10 9
```

South opens third in hand with a light One Spade and obtains the contract in Three Spades. West holds the first trick with ♡ Q and leads a second heart. South puts on the Ace from dummy, ruffs a heart, and plays Ace and another spade.

To avoid being left on play later, West goes up with the King and exits with a spade. Declarer finesses ◇ Q and West is in with the King. The problem now is, should West exit passively with a diamond or should he try to grab a couple of club tricks?

Count the declarer's winners. He is known to have four spade tricks, one heart and, if you return a diamond, three diamonds. Conclusion, you don't need to be 'busy'; just return a diamond and wait for two club tricks.

There is another way of looking at it. South can be counted for six cards in the minor suits. However these are distributed, the discards on diamonds won't help him.

In a final example the defence emerges victorious.

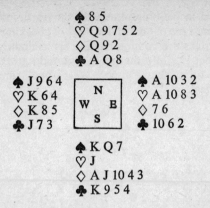

```
                    ♠ 8 5
                    ♡ Q 9 7 5 2
                    ◊ Q 9 2
                    ♣ A Q 8
    ♠ J 9 6 4          N          ♠ A 10 3 2
    ♡ K 6 4       W        E      ♡ A 10 8 3
    ◊ K 8 5           S          ◊ 7 6
    ♣ J 7 3                       ♣ 10 6 2
                    ♠ K Q 7
                    ♡ J
                    ◊ A J 10 4 3
                    ♣ K 9 5 4
```

South opened One Diamond, North responded One
Heart, and South rebid One No Trump. North raised to
Two No Trumps and South went on to game.

West led the 4 of spades, East won with the Ace and
returned the 2, indicating a four-card suit. South crossed to
♣ Q, led ◊ 9 from dummy and followed with the Queen,
losing to West's King.

West could have cleared the spades now, but he paused to
count South's hand. His partner had played high-low in
diamonds, suggesting a doubleton, and the 2 of clubs on the
first round of that suit. It looked as though declarer was
3-1-5-4 and he could hardly have the Ace of hearts.

If the defence had needed four tricks from hearts West
would have led low at this point, playing his partner for
A J 10 x. But only three hearts were needed to beat the
contract and South might hold the singleton Jack. Having
reached this conclusion, West laid down the King of hearts
and followed with another.

The epigram that anyone who can count up to thirteen
can be a bridge expert is not far wide of the mark!

Index

Bridge for Beginners 50p
Victor Mollo and Nico Gardener

This excellent book is for the complete beginner. It explains every phase of bridge step by step – the rules, scoring, the conventions and techniques of bidding and card play. And there are exercises after each lesson to help the reader develop his newly acquired skill.

Common-Sense Bridge 50p
Rixi Markus

Although good technique is essential for a player of championship class, something much more personal is also needed – a bridge philosophy.

Internationally acknowledged as one of the world's greatest players, Rixi Markus expounds on her own ideas and those adopted from great masters.

Using illustrative hands to take the reader through every aspect of bidding and play, she shares her remarkable insights to produce a sure signpost to better and more enjoyable bridge.

'Excellent hands [and] good material . . . it will certainly make you think' FINANCIAL TIMES

'Most enjoyable reading' THE SCOTSMAN

The Pan Book of Card Games 50p
Hubert Phillips

Outstanding – no other book of card games explains so many games so thoroughly or offers so much instruction.
50 card games and
28 games of patience
This famous work with its lucid descriptions and its innumerable specimen hands played out card by card will afford hours of entertainment.

'A fine book' OBSERVER

300,000 copies already sold in Pan

The Complete Patience Book 50p
Basil Dalton

Here are three best-selling Patience books for the price of one!
Incorporating the author's *Games of Patience*, *Double Pack
Patience* and *Patience Problems and Puzzles*, it includes over one
hundred different games of Patience. Some are easy, some are
difficult – all provide a unique form of mental exercise and
entertainment.

Play Poker to Win 60p
Amarillo 'Slim' Preston with Bill G. Cox

Reading Slim's book is like looking over his shoulder at the card
table for a personal lesson in winning.
He explains in detail the strategy and tactics of poker, how to bet,
how to gauge the opposition's strong and weak points, when to
bluff, when to drop and when to pick up your chips and head for
home.
For all Slim's hard-nosed advice and fantastic success, his
narrative is unassuming, quick-paced and spiced with colourful
anecdotes of big-time gambling.
Slim doesn't merely play the cards, he plays the people holding
the cards. He plays to win – and so can you.

Gerald Abrahams
The Pan Book of Chess 40p

'Has the huge advantage over most primers that although it
gives the basic elements, it interests itself right from the start in
the strategy and tactics of the game rather than in mere to-ing and
fro-ing. It will thus advance the tyro far faster than most'
LIVERPOOL DAILY POST

'Offers much value for little money . . . The key chapter, nearly
100 pages long, contains much common-sense on tactics, strategy
and positional judgement, as well as copious examples from
master practice, shrewdly selected for lapses no less than sparks
of genius' NEW STATESMAN

'Will be greatly enjoyed by anyone who likes to see the play of a
highly intelligent and well-stocked mind over the chess scene'
THE SUNDAY TIMES

Test Your Chess 50p

55 problems by one of Britain's leading exponents of Chess.

'What I do offer to the Chess public is a collection of studies, in
the attacking of most of which all degrees of players will get some
result, and will be able on studying (later, I hope) the answers, to
measure their actual skill' FROM THE PREFACE BY GERALD
ABRAHAMS

Oswald Jacoby & John Crawford
The Backgammon Book   £1.00

'THE BIBLE OF THE GAME' NEW YORK POST

A complete, up-to-date, step-by-step guide on how to play
backgammon for love or money – and win.
Written by two world champions and illustrated with large,
precise diagrams, this essential guide ranges from the crucial
opening moves to the finer points of the middle and end games.
Simple, clear instructions and authoritative analyses will entice
the beginner and benefit the expert.
In addition to probability tables, etiquette and the official rules
of the International Backgammon Association, there are chapters
on the history of the game, how to run a tournament and how to
play chouette (backgammon for more than two people), plus a
useful glossary.

'Written by enthusiasts for enthusiasts . . . it will raise the
standard of play' THE ECONOMIST

'I can't remember a book that makes learning a new game more
alluring or easier' SPORTS ILLUSTRATED